EMPOWERING

Life

SKILLS

FOR TEEN GIRLS

Succeed in School, Build Strong Relationships,
Manage Emotions, and Conquer Puberty

MARIA DAWN

Special Art

Empowering Life Skills for Teen Girls

Succeed in School, Build Strong Relationships, Manage Emotions, and Conquer Puberty

Published by Special Art Books
www.specialartbooks.com

Paperback ISBN: 9791255531494

Cover Illustration by Maria Francesca Perifano
Image Credits: Shutterstock

TABLE OF CONTENTS

Part 2: Building Healthy Relationships

Part 3: Academic and Future Success

Part 4: Global Citizenship and Entering the World Stage

FOREWORD

For Parents and Educators (Teens, Turn the Page ...)

Being a teen girl is both an exciting time and a time of uncertainty. So much information is available about *how* to be a teen, but with that comes conflicting messages for girls. How do they navigate the turmoil of emotions sparked by puberty? How do they find who they are and become comfortable with their own identity and body image in the sea of comparison, sometimes at a fever pitch on social media? How do they manage relationships that become increasingly complex? How do they plan for their future?

Teen girls need a trusted roadmap for learning and applying key essential life skills. That is why I am pleased to introduce *Empowering Life Skills for Teen Girls: Succeed in School, Build Strong Relationships, Manage Emotions, and Conquer Puberty*. With its tone of positivity and resilience, topics are handled in an age-appropriate, supportive manner to give girls credible, reliable information in a way that is engaging and enjoyable.

Over my three decades as a psychologist, child developmentalist, educator, and parent coach, my overarching goal has remained the same—to promote optimal outcomes for kids. I believe the most powerful way to do this is to bring research into practical application. Through the translation of key concepts into relatable, actionable guidance, this book accomplishes this beautifully and provides a dynamic, well-considered resource to supply teen girls with the life skills they need to flourish and come into their own.

Drawing on her diverse and inspiring professional and personal background, Maria Dawn achieves this through humor, storytelling, and deep insight to blend the topics that matter to teen girls with meaningful, real-world applications through relatable scenarios and examples. *Empowering Life Skills for Teen Girls* also sparks self-awareness and reflection to help girls look within to find their own path forward.

Rather than a dry, dull list of what to do and what not to do, the book addresses the key areas so crucial for independence and reaching personal goals in a manner that is deeply engaging. From biology to psychology, these essential life skills include navigating emotions, personal empowerment, body positivity, creating healthy relationships, setting goals and planning for the future, and being a good global citizen.

I commend Maria Dawn for harnessing her considerable skill and commitment to educating and mentoring teen girls in this authentic and comprehensive guide. I enthusiastically endorse *Empowering Life Skills for Teen Girls* as a vital resource to guide girls in their journey to understanding, appreciating, and mastering the challenges of adolescence. As a supportive, non-judgmental guide to navigating what can be a complex, frequently confusing road, the message that comes through loud and clear is one of hope, joy, and empowerment.

Sincerely,

Lilla Dale McManis, MEd, PhD

Psychologist and Educator

INTRODUCTION

To the Teenagers—Yes, You!

The teenage years often come with a sense of panic.

Oh, no. A PIMPLE! Why can't your skin just stay as nice and smooth as a baby's for life? Why do you have to deal with nasty spots all over? Not to mention, hair starts growing in weird places and you bleed once a month. Is that *really* necessary?

Well, it's part of being human! And it signals the change to adulthood which should be celebrated. You're on your way to becoming an adult—a woman (if you identify as female)! And as an adult, you're about to embark on your own life—a life that you can consciously choose to create to your liking.

But why are you panicking about all the small things? It's just a pimple, or a hair. Whatever. Only you feel like the world has come to a sudden end.

That's the teen mood swings for you. For some, things seem less drastic as the mood swings are barely noticeable, for others it feels like what used to be a walk in the park has turned into a rollercoaster ride and you barely recognize yourself anymore. You *feel* different. And what you think and feel about others might be changing, too. Not just because you're changing, but because they're changing.

In short, your hormones are going a bit crazy as they transform you from child to adult. That's why you feel like everything's great one moment and everything's a disaster the next. Plus, you're stepping into your own—becoming your own person and that involves a bit of change. That's why some friends tend to fall away at this time in your life. You suddenly realize you don't have that much in common anymore.

It can be confusing. Downright terrifying at times. Change often is. But as with the caterpillar turning into a butterfly, it's possible to transform into something *beautiful*. And the journey itself can become rewarding if you only know how to stay grounded and learn to enjoy the ride.

But wait, there's more.

As you grow up you also experience new things. Like falling in love. It's not about you turning into a butterfly, but the butterflies in your belly.

Falling in love can be overwhelming at first—all those new emotions and suddenly thinking you simply *have* to spend time with this or that person. But love, essentially, is a beautiful thing. Once you dig through the layers of attraction, find lasting love, and create a healthy relationship with someone or several someones (we don't always hit the jackpot right off the bat), it becomes beautiful.

It's just that, unlike what the romance novels and rom coms would have you believe, love isn't just something that stays just because you find it. You have to *build* great relationships with friends, family, and partners.

And then, there's all the adulting. How do you take care of your finances? Map out a path to a career that you love *and* which serves you financially? How do you best take care of your body and mind? How do you make a good impression and win at networking in the adult world?

In short, you're learning to stand on your own two feet. That alone can feel like a lot, never mind your emotions running amok and your body transforming.

BUT, as always, there's gold—as an adult, you will have to take responsibility for your life and actions, sure, but you also have the *freedom* to do whatever you like. You can start creating a life that makes you excited to wake up in the morning! The kind that has you singing on top of your lungs for no reason.

So, again, there *is* treasure at the end of the rainbow.

And this book is all about discovering it.

First of all, knowledge is power—we (or I, but I work with a team of editors and publishers) will teach you about puberty and the changes you're going through. We will teach you how to find your own inner calm. How to figure out what you're really thinking and feeling so you don't get led astray by teenage hormones. It can be hard to stay calm. Especially if people around you are acting out. But as you'll come to see, you have a choice. You can act as *you* want to act, no matter how the people around you are acting.

Secondly, we will help you understand how great relationships are forged. What the difference between love and attraction is, as well as how you can actively work to create beautiful relationships with *all* the people in your life.

Lastly, we will teach you about the practical stuff, like finances, career paths, and all that jazz (but we will make it more fun than what it sounds like for those who aren't too keen on financial management).

We will do all of this with as much humor, compassion, and wit that we can muster. Because frankly, without those, life becomes pretty dull!

And if there are chapters you find challenging, concepts you just don't understand—ask an adult whom you have faith understands you and can guide you to help explain them. We're all different and we all see the world differently, and as a result, we read different things into the things we read (yeah, that got convoluted!). But my point is: it sometimes helps to have a second pair of eyes look at something and explain it to us.

As I'm neither a physician nor a psychologist and cannot give psychological or medical advice nor diagnose anything, I can only share my own thoughts and learnings—including research-based learnings backed up by studies—so if you feel that there are things you need to talk to a professional about, please approach them. All medical professionals keep information confidential and can be of help in areas where friends and family can't.

Now, let's have some fun as we deep dive into puberty and adulting—enjoy the read!

Maria Dawn

Who am I?

You're reading my book, so here's a little about me.

I'm Maria. I've lived in seven countries on three continents and trained as an actor, director, and producer. I also became a life coach because I love personal development, and acting gave me great insights into psychology. I unexpectedly slipped into writing—crafting copy, content, and books, especially in self-help, relationships, and health.

As a digital nomad, I traveled extensively. In South Africa, I joined an NPO focused on education and have been an honorary director for over a decade. Through this, I raised three kids from the local township, learning a lot about parenting and neurodiversity.

Throughout my life, I've been on a quest to learn how to live better, have more fun, and assist others in doing the same.

PART 1:
Understanding Yourself

1 NAVIGATING EMOTIONS

Emotions can be overwhelming in our teens—suddenly hormone storms seem to appear out of nowhere, and we feel all sorts of things. How do we deal with that? What are emotions? And are our emotions always true? Let's find out!

✳ Developing Emotional Intelligence

When it comes to emotional intelligence (often referred to as EQ), you could say there are two areas: how good you are at understanding your own emotions and how good you are at understanding other people's emotions.

In this chapter, we talk only about *your* emotions. Those wonderfully weird little things that can make you feel like you can take on the world or feel like you are smaller than an ant ... all in the same day!

The thing with emotions is that they often cloud our view of reality. Or perhaps I should say: they *always* cloud our view of reality.

When we feel great, we see everything through rose-tinted glasses. We're super thankful for a serving of ice cream and think the Queen herself (if you happen to have one in your country) couldn't be more grand and regal than we are, so we're totally going to rock the next event we're attending.

When we're feeling down, we think it's just a serving of ice cream (who cares?) and we are some mousy little thing who'd look totally misplaced at any event.

Thankfully, once we become aware of how our emotions shape our view of reality, we can learn to see a bit clearer.

We also learn that perhaps we shouldn't act on something when we're so happy we feel over the moon or so down that everything seems totally wrong.

Why not act on something when you're incredibly happy?

Well, you should definitely act on things when you're feeling *good* about yourself and life. That's fine.

The problem comes when you feel over the moon. That's when you decide to head five school organizations, clean Aunt Clara's house and walk her two dogs for a week, and do all that on top of homework, friends, family time, and downtime. We become impulsive and overly optimistic/ assertive when we feel so happy we could fly (case in point: we cannot fly).

On the flip side, when we're feeling down, we think we can't do anything.

Let's say you're feeling a bit down on a day with soccer practice. Your coach gives you some feedback, saying you need some extra practice if you want to play in the finals. This is a good thing, right? With some extra practice, you'll make the finals!

Only, you're feeling down, so you start crying, thinking you might as well give up soccer. If you need *extra* practice to play in the finals, you must be a terrible player! Feeling down in the dumps, perhaps you will throw in the towel then and there and stomp off saying you quit soccer.

Of course, you'll regret it in the morning when your brain chemicals have become more balanced after a good night's sleep (more about sleep in another chapter). And that's when you have to come crawling back to your coach and tell them you made a mistake.

Not fun. It's better *not* to deal with just about anything until you feel grounded, although some things have to be dealt with in the moment. Later on in this book, we will look at how to ground ourselves in the moment, but for now let's stay on the topic of "heated emotions."

Anger is another emotion to watch out for. Most people know they shouldn't speak or do something rash when angry, because they'll regret it later. Going for a walk before responding to an email that upset you is a very, very good idea.

The thing is, no one *wants* to wait to act. Especially when they're angry. When you're raging, you won't feel like sitting down to meditate or going for a walk before responding to that horrible email you just got. But waiting to act is exactly what you should do if you want to write a response that gets you the outcome that you want.

Anger can fuel us on, which is good if used productively. So instead of responding to whatever makes you furious, go do something else that needs to get done. No one cleans the house as fast as an angry person! Then write a response to the email once you've figured out what you want the outcome of that response to be—do you want them to see your fury, or do you want to achieve something else? If you want to achieve something else, how do you need to phrase your email to achieve that?

If you want to win in life, you're going to have to learn to see that your emotions are just that—emotions. Chemicals triggered by thoughts or events. Emotions will pass. You won't feel the way you do forever. Even if you don't think that's possible when you feel like your heart has been shattered, or you want to kick down a wall because you're so angry.

Don't worry, we will learn techniques for taming the beasts called emotions. Plus, we will learn how to create and harness good emotions— the ones that make you feel great without giving you an emotional high that will lead to a crash.

KEY TAKEAWAYS

- Emotions cloud your view of reality.
- Over-the-top happiness can make you impulsive.
- Feeling down can lead you to underestimate yourself.
- Anger often causes regretful reactions.
- Always consider what you want from a situation before acting—wait until you're level-headed to communicate effectively.

✳ Thoughts, Emotions, and Reality

I feel therefore I am. But is what I feel true?

Let's look at an example.

You are on your way to a small party with friends. It's early evening in summer. It's hot. So you decide to have a chocolate ice cream. Yum. Only, someone bumps into you, and you spill the ice cream on the front of your shirt.

Uh-oh. Suddenly you panic, thinking about the fact that the person you have a crush on will be at the party. What are *they* going to think? Are they going to laugh at you? After all, you look like a toddler who just had an ice cream, not a teenager.

You start feeling embarrassed just thinking about it! Suddenly, the party you were looking forward to doesn't seem all that appealing. Perhaps you should just go home? After all, the person whom you have a crush on probably isn't interested anyway. And you had an argument with one friend last week, and even if you have sorted it out, they probably don't want you at the party tonight.

You feel deflated and want to go hide under a rock. In fact, you consider turning around and going back home. There's always Netflix, after all.

Uhm, what just happened here? You painted a very vivid picture of a scenario that hasn't happened yet. That scenario made you *feel* things.

Let's say that exactly the same thing happens (you spill some ice cream all over yourself while on your way to a small party with friends), but you think, "OMG that's hilarious. I look like a toddler who had ice cream. This is going to be a great topic of conversation all night. Well, hopefully not all night. I'm sure someone has something else I can borrow and wear instead. Either way, I'm gonna have a good laugh about this with a great deal of people."

You feel elated, laughing at what happened. You imagine the perfect evening—filled with laughter and silliness.

Happily you go to the party, and when you arrive, you start cracking jokes about how you spilled ice cream all over yourself, before borrowing some clothes from the girl who's having the party.

So here you can see how you can feel two different feelings that are pretty much the opposite, even though in reality only one thing happened: you spilled your ice cream on your shirt.

Therefore, are your emotions real or are they just a product of what you're thinking? The latter, right? If you think happy thoughts, you feel happy; if you think sad thoughts, you get sad.

Thoughts and emotions aren't necessarily based in reality. Everyone sees the world and events differently and, therefore, has different thoughts. How you see yourself, how your gran sees you, how your friend sees you, how your enemy sees you, and how your teacher sees you are all different. Thoughts are simply an interpretation of reality.

Emotions can be triggered by thoughts. If you think of all the things about yourself that you're proud about, you feel good. If you think of all the things that you don't like about yourself, you feel sad, down, or bad. Therefore, thoughts determine *some* of our emotions.

Our own biological makeup also determines how we feel. Having more of one chemical, hormone, or neurotransmitter than another means you might be more prone to feeling happy or sad, get upset or excited more easily, and so forth. Our nervous system at large and other biological factors can also play part in our emotions—it's a complex topic.

We all have different chemical makeups. That also means we have different neural pathways.

The good news? There are tips for how to balance your brain chemicals and improve your mood (get more of the "happy" chemicals).

There are also ways to *think* about things that help you feel better. Such as thinking that a chocolate stain is a great conversation starter instead of the beginning of social ruin!

There are simple ways to think about situations that can help you feel better about them—such as asking yourself how you can turn it around to something positive.

Can you remember a situation like this where you could have chosen to think about things differently?

KEY TAKEAWAYS

- Your perspective shapes your feelings and actions.
- When faced with negativity, pause and ask if you can view the situation differently.
- Look for lessons or ways to turn negatives into positives.
- The more you practice this, the easier it becomes.

✳ The Really Real Events

Imagining things differently is great, but what about the *really* real stuff?

Let's say you did go to that party with a chocolate-stained shirt and someone made fun of you, which had the person you really like laugh at you, then walk away. You spend the entire night thinking your social life is ruined and you'll never live this down at school. Plus, the person you really like will *never* date you now.

A tad melodramatic? Perhaps. But that's what teenage emotions are often like.

The cure? Think about all the things that are going right in your life—things you're good at and your achievements, no matter how small. Then think of the friends and family you have that love you regardless of a chocolate stain. And, come to think of it, people who judge based on trivial things (like chocolate stains) are being pretty silly and aren't worth your concern.

I know, it's not that simple. People in school listen to some people. And it's not nice if those people turn against you.

> But you have to decide how you see yourself, how you feel about yourself, and which people are truly worth keeping in your life.

You decide whose opinions matter and whose opinions don't. The most important opinion that counts? Your own. So decide to look upon yourself in a positive light.

And this isn't just about big events; it's about everything in your life. You can decide you're stupid because you failed at math and feel horrible about being you, but are you really stupid? Or is that just a story you're telling yourself? What about all the things you got right?

> Count the stuff you do well, not the stuff you do wrong.

I used to think that because I don't have a mom (she died when I was six), I don't know how to be a woman. But there were lots of women around me, and I was born into a woman's body which I felt totally at home in, so of course I knew how to be a woman. I probably knew better than most people how to be a woman because I had two grandmothers helping to raise me!

If you only have one parent or no parents, if a parent is on drugs or in prison, or if your parents don't understand you, it doesn't make you lost or unlovable—it makes you strong and courageous.

You need to learn to flip the switch, so to speak. If you suddenly feel your mind going dark with negative thoughts, you have to start asking yourself if the story you're telling yourself is true. Is it helpful? Is it kind? Or could you think something about yourself, your life, or the situation you're in that'd make you (a) feel better or (b) act better? Pay attention to the stories you tell yourself.

Create powerful and loving stories. Need inspiration? Look up stories about people in similar situations. Look for support groups that talk about the specific situation you're in. This is one thing social media is very good for.

Here's another point: sometimes we need help or information to change the way we view a situation. Like a psychologist or therapist helping us out.

Other times, we need help to get out of a situation. For example, you can choose to see yourself differently from how the bullies see you but you still need to get out of being bullied. Either the bullying has to stop or you need to somehow remove yourself from the situation. You can't just say, "Well, I could learn from this that other people's opinions don't matter and be happy anyway." Yes, you can do that, but you also have to get away from it as it can be dangerous for your mental and physical health.

If you are in any kind of danger, if you're being bullied, or if there's some other situation that you don't know how to handle, you need to (a) seek information and (b) get support so that you can either get away from the situation or change the situation.

Let the negative events in your life be catalysts for positive change.

When something negative happens, I tell myself, "This is the best thing that ever happened to me," so that I have a shot at finding the gold in the situation.

That might sound absolutely ridiculous, but let's say you're diagnosed with type 2 diabetes. That is, by all accounts, a bad thing. But let's say you get cured from diabetes, and in the process, you learn to live a healthier life that also makes you happier. What's more, during treatment, you meet the love of your life, decide to become a medical doctor who cures other people of diabetes, and even work to find a cure for diabetes type 1.

Seeing good in bad situations doesn't mean you ignore the difficulty. It just means you open the door for something good to come from it. You might be scared, angry, or sad, but this positive mindset will help you to start looking for the good.

I've often thought, for example, that if something ever happens to my best friend, I'm toast. But as her kids' godmother, I'd have to find the good somehow to be able to help them. I would have to believe that something good could come out of a horrible situation, or I'd sit down, cry, and not move a muscle. That wouldn't make the situation "good."

When we look for the good in the bad, it doesn't mean we won't be upset, sad, angry, or whatever it might be. It just means we realize there's more to life than our present pain. When we look for the good, we often find it.

Life isn't always happy, or good, or even kind. But there are happy, good, and kind moments and people. So when something difficult happens, it's important we stay open to the possibility of something good coming from a heart-wrenching situation.

This is all well and good to talk about in theory, but it's really difficult to practice because our emotions can feel absolutely overwhelming. It's so important to shift our focus, and be as stubborn as possible when it comes to looking for good things to come out of bad places and situations!

Remember: you can decide how you see yourself and your life and therefore how you feel about yourself and your life. That's your power. Don't let anyone take it away from you.

No one can make you feel inferior without your consent. - Eleanor Roosevelt

KEY TAKEAWAYS

- How you see yourself and events shapes how you feel.
- When bad things happen, focus on your strengths, achievements, and the people who care about you.
- In harmful or negative situations, seek information and support to make necessary changes.
- Don't delay taking action if something is harming you mentally or physically.
- Question the negative stories you tell yourself and seek new perspectives.
- Building happiness and a life you love takes work, but it becomes easier with practice.

✳ Know Thyself ... and Improve Yourself!

Some people are really good at taking charge of their emotions "in the moment." When something happens, they take a breath, recalibrate, and act completely calmly.

Other people, whether due to past events, how they saw others handling situations when they were small, or chemical makeup, can't do that. They might become overwhelmed by anger or start panicking.

In a previous example, I talked about spilling ice cream all over yourself before a party and choosing to see it in a fun light—it's going to be a great conversation starter (as opposed to shying away, thinking everyone will ridicule you).

However, you might not, at this point in time, be able to do that. Perhaps, you don't have the social skills yet. Perhaps, you easily get upset. Perhaps, you need to plan things, and if things don't go according to plan, you feel anxious.

We're all different. And while, with time and practice, you can overcome a lot of things that make you nervous, anxious, angry, etc., that might not be where you're at right now.

That's fine. What you have to remember is to put yourself first. If you feel you can't face a party while wearing a dress covered in chocolate, then don't do it. While it's good to challenge yourself, if you know you're not going to be able to shrug it off and use the ruined dress as an excuse to crack jokes, then don't attend the party.

You need to feel safe within yourself when you do something. And to do that, you need to build your confidence. But first, let's look at some situations that might act as "emotional triggers" that make you anxious and how to not necessarily remove the triggers, but learn how to deal with them.

I've traveled the world and find it really strange that people feel lost in new places—I just ask for directions and figure things out as I go. But many people feel completely overwhelmed by that and want to go hide under a rock! For them, being lost is a trigger.

On the other hand, I find negative comments about my work and, especially, my personality daunting. I have to really step back and acknowledge that while the criticism could be correct, it's not a measurement of my worth.

So how do we "neutralize" our triggers so that when things happen we don't go into reaction mode?

Sometimes we can set up safe environments for us to act things out in. With my little one, I sometimes roleplay things. For example, he used to have an issue at the playground with taking people's toys. He was too scared to ask, so he just took them instead. So at home, we acted this out—I pretended to be a child, and he asked to play with my toy.

He also gets very angry if someone accidentally hurts him or upsets him, and instead of lashing out, he needs to tell a teacher. So we have acted that out.

You can act out situations yourself by imagining something happening and then reacting to it. You can also do this as a mind movie (as opposed to acting it out). In fact, when I was in drama school our principal encouraged us to do this—he called it "foreburning."

Let's say you have an audition. You often get nervous at auditions. As a result, your acting isn't as good as it could be. So for your next audition, you practice in your mind. Every day, you close your eyes and imagine being at the audition. You feel your nerves, acknowledge them, and then concentrate on how you want to feel—relaxed. You're taking deep breaths and, stepping into the role of the character, seeing the world through her eyes. You also imagine that the people holding the audition want you to succeed—they want to find the right person for this role.

You do this every day until it becomes second nature.

Then, let's say you go to the audition and everything goes well until one of the people who are judging your performance says it's not what they're after and asks you to do it differently.

You freeze. You haven't planned for this. And the person criticizing you is looking at you expectantly but also with doubt. They doubt you. This isn't going to work out. You feel panic bubbling up. But you remember to acknowledge your feelings, take a breath, and get into character. Only you haven't planned for a different interpretation of the character and, as a result, you don't quite nail it. In fact, you do a pretty bad job of it.

You come home feeling deflated, but instead of giving in to despair, you consider you've learned a valuable lesson—things don't always go as planned. How will you act the next time someone criticizes you and/or asks you to do a different interpretation? Or perhaps asks you to try out for another character entirely?

You close your eyes and imagine the audition you just had. Only now, you imagine how you wish you'd acted. And by doing so, you're creating a different neural pathway for next time this happens.

We can all rethink our reactions, be it to how we feel when we're handed a test we need to do, or how we wish to react when someone yells at us.

This doesn't necessarily happen overnight. We need to practice. What also helps is the mood boosters explained in the next section as they help you stay level-headed even when things get difficult.

If you get really emotional, suffer from panic attacks, or have anxiety, you should speak with a psychologist or other medical practitioner before trying out some of these exercises.

You know yourself, but for some things, it's just good to have a professional to help us along if we're unsure we can deal with it … or a bit too sure we can deal with it!

KEY TAKEAWAYS

- We all have different emotional triggers, such as changes in plans or fears.
- Rehearsing stressful events in your mind can help you prepare for how you'd like to respond.
- Mental rehearsal involves imagining the stressful event (or re-imagining it if it already happened), acknowledging your emotions, and practicing a balanced response.
- You can also act things out in real life, such as practicing how you wish to feel during presentations or responding calmly to unpleasant remarks.
- Gradually test yourself in real-world situations within a safe environment.
- If you have PTSD or similar challenges, consult a medical professional before trying these exercises.

✳ Chemical Emotions and How to Take Charge of Them

We're all wired differently. Some people appear to have more "happy chemicals" than others. These happy chemicals include the neurotransmitters serotonin and dopamine. But if you have too much dopamine, you become wired. Kind of like drinking cup after cup of coffee—you can't focus, you can't sleep, and eventually you crash.

Emotions are also funny because you can become addicted to them. Some people get angry easily as it leads to a sort of high with adrenaline (which is actually a stress hormone) pumping around their body and giving them a boost of energy. Other people are scaling rock walls or parachuting to get this kind of feeling. Some people even seek out pain to get a high out of adrenaline.

Serotonin and dopamine can be released when we win at a game, go shopping, or work out at the gym (the two aren't necessarily released together—sugar, for example, leads to the release of dopamine, not serotonin). These chemicals are also released when we take certain kinds of drugs.

In short, we all have a base level. This could mean we feel more happy or more sad than other people.

Neural Pathways and Patterns

In our quest to feel happy, we might get stuck in patterns that aren't helpful. This can range from exercising too much to becoming addicted to drugs. Some people seek out danger or pain; others eat too much ice cream.

Once we go down a certain path, our brain gets used to it. We form so-called neural pathways. Think of it like walking to school. There are three paths you can take, but one is particularly easy so you start walking that one and stick to it. It would require effort to navigate the other paths, so you don't.

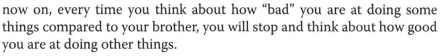

And this also holds true for things that *don't* make us feel good. Such as thinking about what a big loser we are for not being as good as our baby brother at school or at playing soccer.

The good thing? Once you decide to walk a new path and get used to that, that becomes the easy path! So you can decide that from now on, every time you think about how "bad" you are at doing some things compared to your brother, you will stop and think about how good you are at doing other things.

Not only can you learn to take different "thinking routes," there are many healthy ways of improving your mood that require very little thinking! And when you do the healthy things that make you feel good, you're less likely to feel the need to do things that are harmful to feel good (talk about weird—there are bad things that make us feel good!).

Lots of things affect the chemicals in our brain. The things that positively affect our brain chemistry (mood boosters) include:

- Healthy foods (in general whole foods, including plenty of veggies, but also enough of different food groups, such as proteins, fats, and carbs)
- Enough sleep (varies depending on age, but as an adult around 8 hours and as a teen a bit more) on regular hours (i.e. going to bed and waking up around the same time every day)

- Spending time in nature
- Meditation and mindfulness exercises
- Breathing exercises (some refer to it as breath work)
- Physical exercise (especially cardio)
- Social interactions
- Music that makes us feel good

Things that can have a negative impact on our mood are mostly the opposite of what's listed above, but also includes stress, trauma, and abuse of drugs or alcohol.

In short, you can manipulate your brain to produce more of the good chemicals, or simply balance things out, by changing certain habits in your life (or adopting new ones, like exercising for twenty minutes a day and meditating for ten minutes).

What's also really cool is that exercising, learning new things, and having novel (new) experiences with people can help increase our cognitive reserve. That means that when we grow older and some of our synapses might malfunction, we have so many left that our brain still works well.

Now, this isn't a book that goes into science in detail, and I'm not a scientist. While I have written complicated articles looking at the science of happiness, I can positively say that it's really hard to know exactly how your brain will react to something because there are a myriad of different variables. Your genes, your serotonin and dopamine levels, and so forth all play into how you react to different things.

What I do know is that these mood boosters have been scientifically studied, and the more you do things that make you feel better, the less likely you are to have bad mood swings.

Of course, you also have to check your focus. If you keep thinking about the negative aspects of your life, you don't feel great. Shifting your attention, as discussed in previous sections, is really important if you want to learn to manage your state of mind.

A Note on Supplements

While on the topic of improving brain chemistry, I should mention that there are supplements that can help balance your mood. What's really important to remember when it comes to supplements is that they can be powerful. That's great, but it also means that some supplements can't be combined with certain medications. Did you, for example, know that simply eating a grapefruit affects a lot of different medications? While grapefruit comes with a load of health benefits, it interacts with many medications!

Some supplements when combined with medication can, in fact, be lethal. So, please, if you're taking medication or have a condition of any kind, talk to a medical doctor who is well educated in herbalism before taking supplements.

When it comes to supplements, you also have to figure out exactly what supplements will work for you. For example, let's say you are feeling down lately. Perhaps you think your serotonin levels are low, so you buy a supplement to increase serotonin.

Now, there are many different things in your body that happen to produce serotonin and keep serotonin levels high. If you take a supplement that improves one of those biological processes, it might turn out that the supplement doesn't work, because that's not the biological process that you're having issues with.

To increase serotonin levels, you might therefore want to look at different supplements that support serotonin levels in different ways.

Yet other supplements might increase serotonin levels no matter what as they block serotonin receptors, meaning serotonin is floating around in your brain for longer. In fact, that's how some antidepressants work (though I'm not sure if there are supplements that do the same).

Then again, it might be your dopamine levels that are low, not your serotonin levels. What I'm trying to say is that unless you know what's wrong and why, it's not always easy fixing it.

What's more, some supplements can have adverse effects. Or, if you have some other condition, it could make that condition worse, even if it helps with what you are taking the supplements for. This is why it's crucial to speak with a healthcare practitioner before you start experimenting with supplements.

Herbal teas and tinctures also fall under the category of supplements, though teas are usually weaker in strength. I'm a lover of herbs and find the power of plants fascinating, and for that reason, I know that seeking expert advice is a really good thing.

KEY TAKEAWAYS

- Everyone has a unique biological makeup that influences how they feel and react to emotions.
- We can improve our mood by establishing routines that support brain function.
- Try these mood boosters:
  - Eat a varied, whole foods diet rich in vegetables.
  - Exercise for 20 minutes daily.
  - Spend time outdoors, preferably in nature.
  - Practice breathing exercises or meditation.
  - Maintain a regular sleep schedule.
  - Listen to uplifting music with positive lyrics.
  - Spend time with friends and family.
- Some people use supplements to improve mood. Always consult a healthcare professional before trying supplements.

✳ The Stuff That Makes Us Feel Bad

There are lots of things that can make us feel down in the dumps. Let's say you live off fast food, or eat too much sugar. After a while, your brain will become unbalanced, because it won't get all the nutrients it needs to work well. Likewise, if you don't get the exercise you need, or don't spend time outdoors, you can become lethargic or even depressed. This is especially true in winter when we tend to spend more time indoors and there are less hours of sunlight (unless you live in a warm, hot place!).

Things like our social life also affect our mood. Even if you aren't big on social stuff, it's good to have a hobby where you meet other people in a setting that works for you. A book circle, for example, won't put much social pressure on you, but you still interact with others.

The kind of content we consume also affects how we feel. Binging on YouTube or TikTok videos where people talk about how depressed they are isn't helpful. It can be helpful to hear someone talk about depression when we are depressed as it helps us feel less alone. But if the person is talking *about* depression, as opposed to *how to overcome* depression, we might end up in an unhealthy pattern where we fuel our own depression.

If you watch a lot of crime series, listen to songs with negative lyrics, and can't get enough of TikTok videos by teens who are undergoing trauma, you could consider—just for a week—to completely change your "media diet." Watch only feel-good series and movies (that you also enjoy), listen to music with positive lyrics (or no lyrics but with a happy beat/tune such as jazz), and only watch TikTok videos where people explain something useful, talk about something positive, or show how they overcame hardships.

Then there's the stuff we can't always control—stressful events, family changes, or even challenges at school. These can weigh on us and make us feel sad or anxious. If something major happens, like your parents going through a divorce or a close friend moving away, it's important to know that feeling sad is okay. What matters is that we deal with those emotions, acknowledge the other areas of our life, and give them equal attention.

While sadness and mourning are part of life and go away once we've processed our emotions, depression is what happens when we don't process something properly, suppress it, or simply can't stop thinking about it.

Depression can happen because of other things too—as mentioned previously, we all have different brain chemistry to start with and it seems that alone can cause depression and other mental health challenges in some cases.

No one can prevent bad stuff from happening in our lives, but by having daily practices that support our brain chemistry and our mental health, we can help prevent depression. Support systems also play a vital part— from friends and family to therapists who can help us process trauma in a way where we get through it. In fact, I wish everyone who experienced trauma was automatically connected both to a therapist and to a network of people to act as emotional support. It would help us all feel a lot better.

Negative events are part of life, but feeling bad forever doesn't have to be.

What's more, there are the big taboos: drugs, alcohol, and cigarettes. Those are things that can make our brain go completely ga-ga if used irresponsibly.

Having a glass of wine or a cocktail when you're of legal age can be considered responsible drinking. The issue is, with peer pressure and the effect of alcohol itself, we don't always stop there.

Someone gives us another drink. We drink it. Then our judgment starts to go, so when the third drink appears, we no longer think it's a problem. And when someone tells us to drive after the fourth drink, we're so drunk we think it's an excellent idea. Or perhaps we feel a bit tired and decide to nap in the car. In freezing weather. Wearing only a dress.

We can cause a lot of harm to ourselves and others by having "just one more drink."

When you are of legal age to drink, decide up front what your limits are—how many drinks will you drink that day? If someone tries to make you drink more, either say no, pretend to drink but don't, or have a "vodka and cranberry juice" without the vodka. So long as you're having fun, people will have no idea you aren't drinking.

Also, beware when you reach the legal drinking age that while it sounds fine to "have just one drink," if you do it every night, it can become harmful. Again, decide up front what your limit is for the week, not just the night.

As for cigarettes (and this very much includes e-cigarettes), they only cause harm. If someone insists you have them, say no. Or simply say you're into sports. Athletes don't drink or smoke because their performance levels go down.

Vaping isn't as bad as smoking, is it? Well, usually it doesn't contain as many bad chemicals as cigarettes BUT according to the US Center for Disease Control and Prevention, most e-cigarettes contain nicotine which can harm the parts of a youth's brain that control attention, learning, mood, and impulse control.

Maybe that doesn't sound so bad, but have you ever experienced feeling really down? Yeah? Now, imagine you end up feeling down all the time because a chemical in an e-cigarette damaged your brain. Even if it just makes you "a little less happy," is it worth it?

In fact, there are also chemicals in e-cigarettes that can permanently damage your lungs, and there are several cases of death as a result. If you don't already vape, don't start.

But how do people end up addicted to vaping and smoking? Can't you just have a few smokes whenever you're partying, and that's that?

It's not always that easy.

Let's say you "just tried" a cigarette with a friend, then you had a stressful period and realized cigarettes "calmed" you, and before you know it, you're a smoker. The World Health Organization (WHO) estimated that by 2030, eight million people per year will die from smoking.

Meditation or taking deep breaths for five minutes is a healthier way of finding calm when you're stressed. If you're restless, go for a run or walk. Those things will help you feel better *and* improve your overall health. Smoking will not.

Find it hard to motivate yourself to do the good things? Find other people who do them. Set challenges.

Can't find people around you to do challenges with? Join online group challenges. Facebook should sort you out in no time as there are plenty of groups to join (and you can always create a separate account if you don't want to use your regular one for joining groups), but you'll find various other social media platforms where people join wellness challenges, so look on your favorite social platforms, too! There are also plenty of apps you can look into that will help keep you on track.

Peer pressure can be a pain, especially in your teens. So finding other people who help you lead a healthy lifestyle can be incredibly helpful (tip: dancers, sports enthusiasts, and other active people tend to care for their health). Find people who want to get the most out of life and want to feel as good as possible while having as much fun as possible.

The thing with drugs and alcohol is that what seems so innocent can lead to so much harm, and it can happen to anyone.

If you know the pain that addiction causes, it's not worth the experiment.

For an addict, the drug becomes the most important thing in their life, and relationships, life goals, and finances fall by the wayside. Drug addiction affects everyone around the addict.

Are there drugs that can be good if used wisely? Of course. Drugs used to treat medical conditions, prescribed by reputable doctors, can help people heal. It's the misuse and abuse of these drugs that can become a problem. Some people become addicted to pain meds after surgery, for example.

Humans have, most likely, attached shame to addiction because addicts tend to let their lives fall apart due to their number one focus being getting the drug and using it. But addiction itself is simply a biological response to chemical stimuli.

It's not just drugs we can get addicted to, either. Some people are addicted to shopping, food, likes on social media, or even exercising. Basically, anything that makes you feel good can become an addiction; something you can't stop doing even though you know it's not good for you.

If you already know you have an unhealthy pattern with something, or are starting to suspect you do, check in with a professional. To be honest, most of us do one thing or another to "boost our mood" in an unhealthy way (such as binge-watching Netflix instead of dealing with work because work is just too too stressful). But if this thing starts becoming a pattern—something that we do often—it's time to deal with it.

Even if you aren't addicted to something, but simply feel so down you'd like to do anything to get rid of the feeling, ask for help on how to deal with it. Asking for help isn't humiliating—it's life-enhancing.

If you feel insecure about talking to someone, look up what other people with similar patterns have done to beat them. There are success stories when it comes to anorexia, bulimia, over exercising, gambling, working too much … the list goes on. Look up how they did it. Find inspiration. Even if you don't think you need help, look at these stories. They will teach you why breaking the pattern sooner rather than later will serve you and those around you.

And that's another thing—if you develop a negative habit of any kind, it doesn't just affect you, but those around you. Your friends, family, siblings … they all need you in one way or another—whether as a friend, role model, or something else. So if you can't yet face doing something for yourself (like you don't have the motivation), consider doing it for them. Then learn how to do it for yourself.

KEY TAKEAWAYS

- Our brain chemistry can be disrupted by living a sedentary life, not spending enough time outdoors, unhealthy eating, and isolation, all of which can lead to mental health problems.
- Substances like certain prescription drugs and alcohol can impair our ability to think clearly, leading to situations where one drink turns into ten, making us believe we're still sober even when we're not.
- If you recognize unhealthy patterns in your life—such as binge-eating, drinking too much, or compulsively exercising—it's important to seek help from professionals.

- Resources are available, including anonymous hotlines, therapists, psychologists, doctors, and school counselors, as well as online information and inspiring stories to motivate change.
- Remember, there is help out there, others have faced similar challenges and overcome them, and you can too.

✳ Mindfulness—Supercharge Your Brain

There was a time when meditation wasn't very popular. Lately though, meditation has become a "thing" and there's a reason why.

First, let's talk about some misconceptions.

#1 Meditation is a religious practice.

While you can use it as part of a spiritual practice, meditation is a way of calming your brain or, viewed differently, a way of taking charge of your brain. You can meditate simply by slowly breathing in and out through your nose and focusing on that. Some like to close their eyes and focus on what they can feel and hear through their senses.

#2 Meditation requires lots and lots of practice and takes years to learn.

No. See #1—five minutes of breathing every day is a valid way of meditating.

#3 Meditation is super boring.

No. Well, if you sit around trying to think of nothing, it can be. It can also be darn difficult. Because thinking of nothing … well, is that even possible? But if you find sitting still boring, you can do something. Such as working with your breath.

Alternatively, you can listen to a guided meditation, so all you have to do is relax and listen to a story or some meditative music—there's plenty to be found on YouTube. And if you hate doing nothing, why not chant? You'll find instructions for that on YouTube, too.

Being someone who gets antsy myself, I found chanting and breathing to be keys for my meditation practice. Sometimes simply listening or paying attention to my body works well.

But why bother in the first place? What are the benefits of meditation?

Well, because it might:

- Reduce stress, anxiety, and negative thoughts
- Make you more self-aware
- Improve your memory, sleep, and mood
- Improve your immune system
- Slow the aging process

If you want to stay level-headed, improve your focus as well as your mental and physical well-being, and feel better about yourself and the world, I suggest you try meditation.

There are many mindfulness techniques you can try. I particularly like the one where I lie down, then go through each body part, relaxing it. So I think to myself, "I'm relaxing my toes, my toes are completely relaxed," while *focusing my attention on my toes.* Then I move on to my feet, or the soles of my feet, depending on how detailed I want to be. I include internal organs as well. I finish it by saying, in my mind, "I'm relaxing my mind, body, and soul. My mind, body, and soul are completely relaxed."

There are so many different mindfulness exercises, and one of the easiest ways to experiment is to get a mindfulness and/or meditation app.

There's more to mindfulness than meditation. As mentioned, breathing exercises can form part of a mindfulness practice. You don't even have to meditate.

Breathing exercises can be as simple as slowly breathing in and out through your nose, or breathing in through your nose and out through your mouth. You can breathe in on a count of eight, hold for four, breathe out on a count of eight (the counts vary, but you can decide what works for you).

Have a look online to find free breathing exercises to try. If you've never done it before, be sure to have an adult with you in the room as you can get dizzy if you overdo it.

Mindfulness exercises can also include having a diary/journal and recording three things you're grateful for every day.

Think of mindfulness as a way to reclaim your brain from the negative stuff and supercharge it with the good stuff. And just five minutes a day can make a difference. In fact, **I challenge you to try meditating for five minutes before bed or first thing in the morning and see if you notice a difference.**

Another mindfulness exercise to try is to acknowledge how you're feeling and what you're thinking once an hour (set an alarm on your phone), or every time there's a break at school. What's going on in your mind? You can also take a deep breath and feel into your body. Are you tense or relaxed?

It's not just our position that affects our body, but also our thoughts. If we're stressed, worried, angry, or sad, we often tense up. When we check in on our body, we can consciously choose to let go of tension.

As for checking in on our thoughts and feelings—half the time, we aren't even aware of what we're thinking.

Say that again!

Well, you might be doing math. But you feel unfocused, because you're simultaneously worrying about an argument you had with a friend, which is making you fret. Only, you aren't aware of that. You just feel a bit down.

Stopping to check in on our thoughts and feelings can be fascinating. It's also a tool for awareness—learning about what's really going on in our mind. And once you're aware, you have the power to shift things.

Let's say you're feeling down because you had a fight with a friend and now you're worried about your friendship. Take a moment, acknowledge how you're feeling. Really sit with the emotions you're having. Then decide what you're going to do about it. You're going to call your friend after school and apologize. Best case scenario, they forgive you. Worst-case scenario, you've lost a friend. If so, you've learned a lesson and you can now create greater friendships.

Right now, what's the best thing you can do? Think of something positive to put you in a good frame of mind, then focus on math. That will help you get a good grade. Then, at lunch break, you'll consider what you're going to say when calling your friend. As you know it's an emotional situation, you're also going to rehearse the call in your mind on the bus ride home. That way, if your friend doesn't react as you want her/him to, you will be prepared for what to say and how to handle the situation.

We often have a lot of worry and stress, because we haven't (a) faced how we are feeling and (b) decided what to do about different situations. You'll find that your stress about an upcoming test, for example, can be avoided by (a) creating a study plan and (b) doing "mental rehearsal" for how you want to feel on the day of the test.

If you feel emotional about something, challenge yourself to take a breath, count to ten, and imagine something that calms you. If it's a close relative or friend that's making you upset, imagine something they did that was truly loving.

Once you feel calm, respond to what's going on.

And no, that doesn't mean that your sibling turning your room upside down is *right*. It just means that how you respond to it is right. You will feel happy with your actions. And here's the deal—if you want them to understand that they've done wrong and clean up the mess, you are much more likely to achieve your goal by calmly showing them you're upset. They've hurt your feelings. Now, if they want to make you happy again, they should help you clean up.

Stomping your feet and screaming that they are a terrible brother/sister, probably won't have the same effect.

It's hard to remember to take a breath, calm ourselves, and imagine something calming when we're upset. That's why it's good to think of these things in advance if you know something is likely to upset you.

KEY TAKEAWAYS

- Mindfulness practices can enhance the wellness of both your brain and body by reducing stress, anxiety, and inflammation.
- These practices also improve mood, focus, sleep, and memory, among other benefits.
- Mindfulness increases our awareness of thoughts and feelings, allowing us to change negative ones.

WHO AM I AND WHAT DO I WANT?

Up until your teens, you probably didn't think so much about who you are. You like some things, not others. Life's the way it is. Then, suddenly one day, you wake up and question everything. Who are you? Who do you like? Who don't you like? Are the opinions you have really *your* opinions?

Well, let's find out.

✳ Identity

Who are you?

That's the multi-million-dollar question. And up until now you might not really have questioned it. You know you prefer pink to purple and horses to cars … or blue to red and motorbikes to cars. Then, all of a sudden, people start talking about your personality. What career would suit your personality? What friends suit your personality?

What's your personality? And *are* you your personality? Or does personality change? And what about your opinions?

I remember reading Don Miguel Ruiz's book *The Four Agreements* in my twenties and being astonished about how he explained so well that we can believe in two opposing opinions at the same time. This is because, growing up, different people told us different things that we accepted as the truth. When you're five, you aren't going to question what one person or another tells you unless you already have concrete evidence they're wrong.

That means that when Aunt Jessie tells you that you're a shy and withdrawn child because you hide whenever you're around her raucous bunch of kids, you agree. And when Uncle Johnny tells you that you're a bright and outgoing child because you feel comfortable performing theater in front of him and his wife, you agree.

Then, as a teen, when trying to figure out who you are, you realize you think you're both shy and outgoing. Which one is the truth?

Perhaps that's not the best example, as most people are both shy and outgoing depending on the circumstances, but often we buy into things—other people's beliefs—about ourselves and the world. And they can, interestingly, be completely opposing views!

These things can cause conflict. If you believe that people who openly speak their mind are vulgar and people who don't speak their mind are liars, you're going to dislike yourself no matter what option you choose!

I don't know if this makes any sense yet, but in short, growing up, we tend to take on the opinions of others, only to hit our teens and suddenly question everything, including ourselves.

So truly, what is our identity? Well, *it's what we believe ourselves to be*. This could be true or untrue. What you identify with isn't necessarily who you are (some people don't have a lot of awareness of self).

According to *Merriam-Webster*, identity is "the distinguishing character or personality of an individual."

Want another definition? The American Psychological Association defines identity as follows: "an individual's sense of self defined by (a) a set of physical, psychological, and interpersonal characteristics that is not wholly shared with any other person and (b) a range of affiliations (e.g., ethnicity) and social roles. Identity involves a sense of continuity, or the feeling that one is the same person today that one was yesterday or last year (despite physical or other changes). Such a sense is derived from one's body sensations; one's body image; and the feeling that one's memories, goals, values, expectations, and beliefs belong to the self. Also called personal identity."

In short, it is who you believe yourself to be. And sometimes it helps to realize how we see ourselves … and how we'd like to see ourselves. It can help us change any negative views we might have of ourselves.

It can also help ground us—once we know who we want to be, we can act from this place and not feel like a leaf blowing in the wind, not quite sure of who we are or what we want. For example, if you see yourself as an honest person, when Pauline suggests you rob a bank together, you say no … though you might also do that because prison isn't a fun place to be. There are other considerations than who you are when it comes to robbery! And yes, I'm joking, but it is actually a decent example!

So, let's look at who you think you are and things you identify with (such as being a woman, or being good at sports).

Who you see yourself as tends to be made up of:

- Things you love/your interests (horse riding, biking, engineering)
- Aptitudes (drawing, carpentry, singing, math)
- Skills (things you have learned, whether or not you had an aptitude for them)
- Mindset/how you think (strategic, logical, creative, positive)
- Personality traits (shy, outgoing, brazen, talkative, quiet, humorous, brave, curious)
- Gender and sexuality
- Your personal beliefs (politics, religion, morals, etc.)

Some of these can overlap.

For example, you have a natural aptitude for horse riding. It feels like you were born to be in the saddle and it took very little effort for you to learn. But it's also a skill if you practice it regularly.

On the flip side, you might love riding … but found it incredibly difficult to learn. You just stuck with it until you learned enough to be comfortable in the saddle.

Likewise, being creative might come naturally to you, but you can develop it by learning about various creative processes.

On the flip side, you might be born with an aptitude for being strategic and logical, but you aren't particularly creative. That doesn't mean you can't learn creativity.

Personality traits can be ones you're born with, but just as with skills and mindset, you can also develop them. For example, you might be more shy and quiet by nature, but that doesn't mean you can't train yourself to be outgoing.

When it comes to gender, some people are born with one sex, but identify as another. Sexuality is also part of our identity.

Our personal beliefs aren't something we were born with but were raised to believe in. For some, this includes religion. They identify as Hindu or

Christian. Others identify with a political party or a musical style or group. People even identify with certain actors.

Personal beliefs also include how we see the world. "Non-vegetarians are cruel to animals." "Being a vegetarian goes against nature—we were built to eat meat." We also tend to identify with certain things, such as:

- Our personal style (clothes, hair, etc.)
- Where we live (our country and local community)
- Our family and who we hang out with
- Our possessions (cars, home, etc.)

If you feel anything in your identity is holding you back, you can change it.

In our teens we often change a lot. We change friends sometimes. Our interests often change. We question things we previously took for granted (such as the political party our family favors). We discover our sexuality.

This can be a really smooth transition if most things stay the same and our hormones don't cause massive mood swings. It can also be a traumatic transition as we question ourselves and even feel like a stranger to ourselves!

We also tend to be expressive in our teens (and wonder fifty years later why we felt so strongly we had to get that tattoo, or express something that went viral on social media). That usually means using style as a way of expressing ourselves. Suddenly what we wear and how other people perceive us become important to us in a way it never has before.

Perhaps, this is because we feel insecure. Everything is changing, and we're trying to control some aspect of it, or belong with a certain group of people.

Of course, that's not true for everyone. Some teens feel secure in their identity. Others are simply confident in themselves and don't get very attached to what the outside world thinks of them.

The truth is, beyond a core, which would include some things you have a natural aptitude for and some personality traits you were born with, as well as a few things you genuinely love doing, you change throughout life if you expose yourself to new experiences and people and keep learning new skills, as well as educating yourself on different topics.

The moment you understand new knowledge, or learn a new skill, you've changed.

Once you learn this, you tend to be less attached to your outward persona. You also gain confidence as you realize that the mistakes of yesterday are not who you are today. But nor are your victories.

As with anything else, your identity is, in large, a story you've made up about yourself. And that story changes as new information is entered.

Again, it's important you check the story you're telling yourself.

"I had one failed relationship. I learned a lot. These are the main things I learned:_____. My next relationship will be better because of this."

"I had one failed relationship. I'm terrible at relationships. I better stay away from them to prevent disaster."

So what story are you making up about yourself? Who are you?

Whatever you believe in, you'll act on. What's more, whatever you believe will affect your feelings.

Choose stories that empower you.

In fact, why don't you sit down and write down the story of you from an empowering perspective where you clarify, not only who you are and what you like, but why the difficult events in your life have led to learnings and made you a better person! Even if you never before looked at your trials in an empowering light where you thought about your learnings, do so now. Rewrite the story.

KEY TAKEAWAYS

Our identity is made up of various elements, including:

- **Things You Love:** Your interests, like horse riding or biking.
- **Aptitudes:** Natural talents such as drawing or singing.
- **Skills:** Abilities you've learned, regardless of aptitude.
- **Mindset:** How you think—strategically, logically, creatively.

- **Personality Traits:** Characteristics like being shy or outgoing.
- **Gender and Sexuality:** Important aspects of who you are.
- **Personal Beliefs:** Your views on politics, religion, and morals.

We also identify with specific things, such as:

- **Personal Style:** Your clothing and appearance.
- **Where You Live:** Your country and local community.
- **Social Circles:** Family and friends you hang out with.
- **Your Things:** Possessions like cars and homes.

Take time to reflect:

- Write down your interests, aptitudes, skills, and mindset.
- Highlight what you love about yourself in one color and what you'd like to change in another.
- Identify traits you want to adopt and list steps to get there.

✳ You Are Not Your Past

I already touched upon this, but you're not your past.

In the past, things happened. You reacted to those things based on the information available to you at the time and based on your emotional state and thinking patterns.

You're still reacting to the past when you think about it. And you can change those reactions and your thoughts about them.

"I made so many mistakes in my early teens, adulthood will be sure to be a disaster with my track record."

"Thank goodness I made so many mistakes in my early teens—adulthood is sure to be a lot better because I made those mistakes so early on. Now that I have learned from the mistakes, I can move on as an empowered woman."

Check the stories you tell yourself. And check the stories you tell others. Imagine this conversation.

"So, you had lots of friends at your last school?"

"I, uh, no, I was kinda not popular."

Or, you can imagine:

"So, you had lots of friends at your last school?"

"Nah, they weren't my crowd. I'm much happier here."

What picture do you paint of yourself?

And remember, right now, your history is just a thought in your head. It's no longer real. It's over.

Who you are today is not your past, but *you make decisions based on your past experiences.* That's why it's super important to check what stories you're making up about the past!

"I had no friends at my old school, so I'm not even gonna try making friends here. I'm a social failure."

"I had no friends because I was socially awkward. Now I'm taking steps to learning social skills and becoming more confident. Making new friends is becoming easier by the day."

See your past in an empowering light and you become a better person today!

EXERCISE

Take a moment to sit down and think about your history and how you can see it in an empowering light. Like think about the things you have achieved that you're proud of, whether that's a great relationship with your sister or getting a scout badge. Even if you're no longer interested in the scouts, you can still remember the achievement in a positive light!

Then think about certain incidents that you have, perhaps, been beating yourself up about or berating yourself for. Now think about those in a new light. What did you learn? How can you move forward more powerfully now that you have those lessons?

KEY TAKEAWAYS

- Your past is not who you are; it consists of events you reacted to based on your knowledge and emotional state at the time.
- Learn from your past and build your confidence by remembering what went right.
- Extract wisdom from mistakes and difficult situations.
- Take time to think through past experiences that trouble you.
- By viewing your past in a positive light, you learn to see yourself positively. The past is over, and you are constantly evolving.
- Use your past to propel you forward in a positive way, rather than as something to hold on to that defines who you are.

✳ You Are Not Your Emotions

Emotions can blindside us. Imagine this scenario.

You had a bad day at school. You got a test back that wasn't great. You had a disagreement with a close friend. You found out that the school trip you were looking forward to has been postponed. You got a pimple. A big fat red one. On the tip of your nose. And physics class was about some topic you just didn't get and you know there will be a test on it on Friday.

Then you get home and your baby sister just won't leave you alone. You try to study. You really do. You want to understand this physics thing. So you spend much more time on it than normal and finally manage to get it. No thanks to your sister who keeps interrupting you. When you're finally done, you put on some music and lie down to chill for a moment. You need to regain your equilibrium or you're going to snap at your sister, who is still not leaving you alone.

Then your mother comes home and asks you why you haven't done the dishes as you promised. She's clearly irritated after a long day and being stuck in traffic and the last thing she wants is a messy kitchen as now she has to clean that up before making dinner—and she is terribly hungry (or hangry).

At her comment you flip a switch. You've worked so hard with your homework and all she can think about is the dishes? After a day of trials, you shout at her that she understands nothing, she can do her own dishes, after all she's the parent, that's what she should do! If she can't be nice to you after a long day, she's a terrible mother and she deserves to do her own dishes! You hate her, and you tell her so. Then you run into your room, slam the door, and start crying.

Your mother asked a simple question. Sure, she's a bit irritated, but she wasn't terribly rude. She was just … tired. You know that. You know she works hard, sometimes double shifts, to pay the bills. You know she can't relax if things are messy, especially if she has to start cooking in the middle of the mess. You know she loves you. You know she does a lot of the housework and that the dishes are your only responsibility, just like your sister's is vacuuming the floors.

You know that, and yet you told her what you told her. You didn't mean what you said.

What you meant was, "Mom, I've had a long day. I'm tired and irritated, and I haven't had a chance to relax yet as my sister has been a pain in the backside. I know she's got ADHD and can be like that sometimes, but today I needed peace and quiet and I didn't get it. And I still did my best to study, and I finally managed to understand something I'm struggling with. I feel like I should be praised for that, not told off for forgetting the dishes. And now I really need some time to myself to regain my energy before I do anything else, please. I can deal with the dishes when I've recovered."

You're not a terrible person for acting out. You just suffered from emotional overwhelm, which easily happens in our teens.

And it's not always other people we hurt with our comments. Perhaps, instead of getting angry with others, you get angry with yourself. Some people do more than that—they actually do physical harm to themselves. Or they starve themselves or eat too much as a way of trying to control their emotions.

When emotions start to overwhelm you, try to step back before acting on them. Take a moment to breathe deeply. And then acknowledge what you feel and let it go.

Think of emotions like bees swarming in your brain—eventually they will go away and the buzzing emotion you feel will go away with them.

Your emotions don't control you unless you let them.

And even if you are prone to getting upset, angry, sad, or over-the-top excited and doing harebrained things easily, you can change that.

If you don't agree with your actions when you get emotional, you simply have to learn to control your emotions. Chapter 1 dealt a lot with that and you can go back and learn the different exercises.

I am mentioning this as a lot of people beat themselves up about things they did when they got emotional.

Don't.

Emotions are like drugs—they make you do the most crazy things. But that's also why it's so important to either (a) acknowledge the emotion but learn to disassociate and not act on it (think of it as a buzzing in your head that will eventually go away) or (b) do the exercises in chapter 1 that helps us take control over our thoughts and emotions.

At the end of the day, you are responsible for your actions and your actions are influenced by your emotions. That, however, doesn't mean that you know how to control them. You need to take steps to learn that.

If you can't do it on your own, get assistance from a pro. Counselors and therapists, as well as psychologists can help you out.

And don't be ashamed if your emotions or thoughts sometimes go awry. Everybody, at some point in their life, will likely feel like hitting someone. Hard. Possibly throwing them out a window. That doesn't mean we do it. We realize we're emotional. We realize that hitting someone is wrong.

However, for some people, this is more difficult as their emotional and biological makeup is different. That's why it's so crucial to get help if you feel you often desire to do things that might harm you or someone else.

There's no shame in getting help. The opposite is true—if everyone who felt like doing something harmful sought help, there would be very little crime. What's more, we would stop harming ourselves.

Just think about it. Ten or twenty years from now, who do you want to be? What kind of colleague, friend, mother, partner, daughter, sister, or boss do you want to be?

Who you are affects others. By taking charge of your emotional life, whether on your own or with the assistance of someone trained in helping people to do so, you assist others. By being as great as you can be, you positively affect everyone around you.

While you might not choose to act on all your emotions and, therefore, can see you're not just made up of emotions that randomly go off, you still have emotional needs.

We all do. We all want to feel safe (though we might seek unsafe situations if we felt unsafe growing up). We all want to feel loved (though we might reject it if we feel we don't deserve it).

We have other emotional needs, too, and you'll learn more about those and how to satisfy them in chapter 6.

KEY TAKEAWAYS

- Everyone experiences emotions, and acting on them impulsively can lead to regrets.
- Some people are more emotionally sensitive than others.
- If you struggle with emotional reactions, it's important to learn to control or acknowledge them without acting on them.
- Your emotions do not define you; you can observe and choose how to respond.
- If emotions feel overwhelming or negatively affect you or others, seeking professional help can be beneficial for personal growth, even if you don't feel like you're completely out of control.

✳ Sexuality and Gender

A big part of who we are is our gender and sexuality.

As mentioned before, we often start to think more about our identity in our teens. We also, generally speaking, start to think more about sex and dating. Up until this point, not all of us question our sexuality or gender (though some do so at a younger age, which is perfectly normal).

As you're now in your teens, let's look at this a bit more closely.

Some of us are born with the gender we *identify* with. Biologically speaking, I'm a woman. That's the sex I was born with. I also feel like a woman. That means I identify as a woman and am cisgender. Other people are born with a gender they don't identify with—they are transgender or gender-fluid.

Is this normal? Yes.

Being non-binary is nothing new, nor does it only exist in one place—it's simply a fact that some people are born transgender, some cisgender.

Statista found that, "In a global survey conducted in 2023, three percent of respondents from 30 countries identified themselves as transgender, non-binary/non-conforming/gender-fluid, or in another way."

It's normal, yet it can feel extremely difficult if you, as a teenager, don't have anyone who is transgender among your friends and family. That's when joining online support groups, speaking with a counselor, or calling a hotline can be useful. Today, there are also many more stories out there about people who are transgender and you can look them up to seek inspiration.

Gender and sexuality are two different things.

Some people are sexually attracted to one sex, some both sexes, and some aren't sexually attracted to anyone—they're asexual.

You can also be romantically attracted to people. This is different from sexual attraction, and you aren't necessarily romantically attracted to the same gender or people you are sexually attracted to.

Does this sound confusing? It is and it isn't. We're all human, but we have different preferences. Some people like sports, some like art. Some identify as being funny, some as being smart.

It's similar to attraction and gender. We identify as men, women, gender-fluid, or transgender (some Native American tribes have a lovely way of describing this—Two-Spirit . . . at least I think that's a lovely way to put it). We are attracted (or not attracted) to different genders and in different ways (romantically and/or sexually).

The main thing to remember? We're all human and we all deserve the same opportunities, happiness, and freedom. No one should be judged for their gender or sexuality any more than they should for being athletic or smart, or liking apples or pears.

Unfortunately, many people in the LGBTQ+ community have suffered from mental health issues due to fear and discrimination. So if you feel scared or depressed, please do get in touch with someone. You're not alone. You are beautiful.

If you want to find out more about different sexual orientations and gender identities, you can do so from reputable sources online. Even if you are cisgender and straight, learning to respect and use the right terms for other people's gender and sexual orientation is important. For example, Instagram these days lets you put down how you'd like to be referred to (s/he, they/them).

The hardest part might be if you're living somewhere where people have very strong cultural ideas about how people should be. Your culture might not acknowledge that people can be transgender or gay, no matter what biology says. That's hard. It's also hard for people who have been raised a certain way with certain beliefs to see life differently. You have to appreciate how difficult it can be for them (or yourself) if they were raised to see things a certain way.

The most important thing, however, is *how you look upon yourself*. You need to accept yourself for who you are.

What's more, there are many people just like you. And when you're old enough, you can seek them out even if you can't do so right now (though hopefully you can!). For now, if you don't have access to a support network, try to find inspiring stories (books, movies, and more), people to follow on social networks who inspire you, and online support groups. And if you still struggle, either with your gender or sexuality, seek help. There are hotlines, as well as lots of qualified specialists to help you. Hotlines are free, so are many online support groups.

You are you and that's beautiful. Remember that. And take pride in your gender and sexuality. I love being a woman. I love the wisdom passed down among women. I also fully embrace that I was raised by a man and prefer fast cars and cameras to nail polish. I do not understand why anyone would want to spend all their time at salons because I find it an absolute bore. That's not to say I don't like getting my nails done—I do. And I respect that others might want to talk about nail polish trends. It's just that for me, fun is snapping away on a camera, directing a play, or going fishing.

If there's one thing you get from this chapter, I hope it's that you appreciate yourself and others for who they are and seek out stories about people of your gender and sexuality that inspire you. Okay, that was two things … so let's add a third: find other people who accept you for who you are and who are going through what you are right now.

It's not easy, this transition from childhood to adulthood, but it can be beautiful.

KEY TAKEAWAYS

- It's normal to not conform to societal norms; many people identify outside of traditional cisgender and straight definitions.
- If you're struggling to discuss your gender or sexuality, seek online support, read inspiring books, or consult a therapist. Hotlines are also available.
- Cultural differences may make it challenging to feel accepted, but finding a supportive community is crucial for embracing your true self.
- Understand that others' upbringing and values might make it hard for them to see different perspectives.
- If you're straight and have friends who identify differently, ask how they prefer to be addressed. Acknowledgment and acceptance are important, and labels can matter to others.

✳ Deciding on Who You Are

I don't think anyone goes through this life without meeting opposition, troublemakers, and people who are mean to us in one way or another. Perhaps we accidentally caused it, perhaps it just happens. Either way, you will meet people who tell you that you are lacking in one way or another.

First of all, you can't be lacking. You're a human, nothing less, nothing more.

Secondly, you won't ace everything all the time. You have things you're good at, things you're bad at, and you will make mistakes no matter how good your intentions. We all do, because we're not oracles with all the answers.

So, are you going to feel bad about the bad comments, good about the good ones, great about when you achieve things, and terrible when you don't? Or will you see yourself as good for just being (you were born, you're here, it's your birthright) and the rest is a journey where you learn and evolve?

If you're doing your best, learn from your mistakes by asking yourself how you can do better and acquire knowledge on how to be a better human in different circumstances—that's all you can do.

You're not better because you were born with one skill or another. You can, on the other hand, get a lot of joy out of honing your skills and doing something you enjoy.

In short, you're not perfect ... but you're great! And you can decide to do your best and learn throughout life. That makes you a fantastic person.

You also have to make decisions about what we spoke about in the first section of this chapter—your identity. If you are someone who loves horses, then you have to stand up for that no matter what family and friends say. Maybe they don't think it's cool, or they don't think it's practical, or whatever it might be, but if you want to work with horses, that's *your* choice. If you want to fly airplanes instead of getting married and settling down, then that's your choice.

That said, don't disrespect the people who are trying to tell you to do something different. I know what I felt like when I got lecture upon lecture about starving artists and comments like "You could be a news reporter as that's a proper job," when I said I was going to study film. It wasn't fun.

I still remember Grandpa saying, "So, can I be an extra in your movie?" I remember that because he's the only one who did not have an opinion of *what else I should do* instead of film. He accepted my choice. I took a roundabout way and didn't end up working with film right off the bat, but in my Academy Awards speech, if I ever get to do one, he will be mentioned!

The point I was actually going to make is that some of what they said was well-meant. I now understand what it can feel like to "be a starving artist." I understand why I was warned. But the better way of going about it would have been to show me a path where I could earn money *and* be an artist. I eventually figured out how, but it was not without stress, duress, and having a ton of jobs that made me, quite literally, sick to the stomach.

Stand up for what you believe in, but don't disregard what people say. Listen. Understand where they are coming from—their past that made them think the way they do—and acknowledge that you hear them. Perhaps their advice or opinions are misguided, but they are sharing them because of how they were brought up, the life they've lived, and the beliefs they have. And it can be difficult to see outside your own "model of the world" (i.e. how you see the world).

Should someone apply undue force to try to coerce you into a life you don't want (such as forcing you into a certain career path), seek help. There are organizations you can reach out to, and often help can be found at school, too. Either through counselors or teachers who lead extracurricular activities or clubs in the fields you're interested in.

There are other things you have to decide on when it comes to who you want to be, namely *your values,* or personal guidelines. Stephen Covey talks a lot about this in his book *Seven Habits of Highly Effective People* (and his son, Sean, wrote a version specifically for teens!). For example:

Are you a person who stays the course even when things get tough?

Are you a person who does your best?

Are you a person who stays calm in the chaos?

Are you a person willing to give something a go, even if you don't know if you're any good at it?

Are you a person who stays kind (but with firm boundaries), even when people are rude, or unkind?

You can set up these kinds of guidelines and every day repeat them in your mind so that you act on them.

You might not be a person who naturally encourages others, because you weren't raised by parents who were prone to praise and encouragement. Their way to try to get you to do the things they thought good for you was to critique and lecture. So you have to constantly remind yourself to be a person who encourages (if that's who you want to be).

When things get tough, you can stop and ask yourself if you're going to act on the stress or on the guidelines you have.

You won't always succeed. You're human.

But when you know who you want to be, you can find new ways to become that person.

Now, having guidelines for who you want to be, or who you want to show up as, is great. However, sometimes you have to reevaluate. Sure you do the right thing, even in stressful situations, but if those situations get so stressful that they're hurting you, perhaps you have to walk away.

You need boundaries.

Many of us associate who we want to be with obtaining our goals.

There's a lot of talk about being successful. What is that? Is it earning lots of money and hitting career goals, or is it getting up in the morning and enjoying who you are and your life?

No one will be successful at all times. Life will knock you around. You can find your feet over and over again, but if you measure your success in how good you are at getting to x or y goal, you might end up disappointed.

Practicing being who you want to show up as in different situations and getting better at that can be a lot more rewarding than chasing fame and fortune.

That doesn't mean you shouldn't have goals. You should. They add purpose to your life. Just be sure your ego (your self-image) isn't attached to them or that you're just waiting "to live" or "have fun" till you reach a, b, or c destination.

You can live a life full of love, fun, and romance long before you meet the perfect partner.

You can feel sexy, cherished, and glamorous long before you end up on the billboards.

You can feel rich, successful, and smart long before you run a Fortune 500 company.

We think when we hit our goals, we will *feel* a certain way because we will *live* a certain life. My advice? Create that life now. Don't wait for it.

If you want to be a famous actress, get on a stage right now. It can be in your living room and the audience can consist of your best friends, cat, or family. Have friends take headshots and dress to impress when you attend local events. Don't wait for the red carpets to feel like a successful actress.

If you want to run a lucrative business, start selling lemonade (or something a little more inventive) now. Start a local PR campaign, do social media marketing, sell it at markets … whatever you feel like. Drive your beat up Pontiac pretending it's a Porsche. You can be a successful businesswoman right here and now.

A lot of successful people are miserable. Look at how many famous people suffer because they're running after fleeting goals they don't even want. The feeling you're looking for can be created without fame or fortune.

Basically, don't wait for others to label you successful. Don't wait for permission to have fun or for others to tell you that you're glamorous. Allow yourself to feel great right here and right now.

KEY TAKEAWAYS

- Define the guidelines and values you want to live by, so you're not swayed by others' opinions.
- Focus on how you want to show up in situations rather than reacting impulsively; this helps with self-reflection and growth.
- Reflect on your actions after situations, and if needed, seek out knowledge to improve for the future.
- Accept that no one is perfect—learning and course correcting are what truly matter.
- Stay flexible. While persistence is good, recognize when to quit or change direction if something isn't working.
- Principles and values are important, but they shouldn't hold you back or become harmful.
- Don't define your worth by external success. Create joy in the present by acting as if you already have what you desire and engaging in activities that fuel your passions.

✳ What Do I Want?—Finding Your Purpose

Perhaps you feel you have a purpose fueling your life. Like using science to help humanity, creating joy through art, entertaining audiences through storytelling, or building effective machines that improve life on Earth.

Great, you've got that figured out.

Some people don't have a purpose like that—a big driving force underpinned with passion that leaves a positive mark on those touched by it. A more common definition would be: "the reason for which something is done or created or for which something exists," as stipulated by Oxford Languages.

For some people, their purpose is to be a good friend. A good sister, daughter, wife, or mother. A good citizen. A good employee.

Your purpose isn't necessarily to heal the world with your music, entertain the world with your jokes, or save the world with your physics knowledge.

> Your everyday life is filled with purpose, if you only become aware of it.

And while being a good friend might not seem like an inspired purpose—it's not like you sound like the next Gandhi or Mother Teresa when you say it—that's just as important.

I mean, how important are great friends to you? Great mothers (and I don't mean just biological mothers, but mother figures that nurture and share their wisdom)? Great sisters?

Have you noticed how different you feel when you go into a shop where all the shop assistants are happy and helpful and one where they practically sneer at you? Perhaps the people working in the store filled with nice and helpful shop assistants that make you feel welcomed and cherished have it as their purpose to be good shop assistants, and they make a difference in the everyday life of perhaps hundreds or even thousands of people every day.

As humans we tend to feel good when we achieve things. And if you brushed your teeth, went for a run, made your bed, read a book, and cleaned up after breakfast, you achieved things this morning.

Purpose is slightly different. It's something that fuels us. Drives us.

Since I was a kid, I wanted to heal people (or at least help them in some way) and create things, usually arty things. When I write personal development books or health articles, I do both. When I direct plays or films with people in difficult circumstances, I do both. So it makes me happy. But I also challenge myself to say nice things to people, encourage people, be a good mother, be a fun mother, and so forth. And some days, what drives me the most is getting the bills paid! And while it might not be my purpose in life, I love to bake, dance, and make charcoal drawings.

You might have a driving force (or two) that goes beyond the everyday stuff like showing up as a good human, or you might not. What matters is that you have purpose.

So seek your passion. What do you love doing? Horseback riding? Running? Organizing? Cleaning? Studying? Spending time in nature? Researching? Drawing?

Write a list. What are the things you love the most? If there's more than one, can they be combined? You love animals and healing—great, you can become a vet, or someone who works at a horse rehabilitation center or has a home for injured dogs.

Whatever it is, see if you can work it into your life and find a path to walk that allows you to incorporate it. If it gets you out of bed in the morning, that's a great thing.

Even if you find that big driving force, don't ignore the purpose you have in different situations in everyday life.

What I suggest you do is challenge yourself to act with purpose. Don't just show up. Show up as someone who is encouraging, calm, and helpful. Be of service to others. And show up as someone who wants to learn and grow in everything you do—be it building great relationships or building great businesses.

Have a purpose for your actions.

And try setting other goals for yourself as well. Put down three things you want to achieve today like being on time, spending an hour practicing basketball, or going to bed before nine and still having half an hour to read a book.

Keep asking yourself:

- Who do I want to show up as? (referring back to the last section and your guidelines)
- What's my purpose in this situation?
- What are my goals for today?
- What can I do to live my passions today?

Also, just because you don't want to go out and change the world by inventing some new machine, or building a home for orphaned elephants, doesn't mean you can't find purpose in helping a local charity. Or your neighbor. Most people find purpose when they do something that assists others.

Find things to do that make you feel good and that move you.

KEY TAKEAWAYS

- Purpose is a powerful force driven by passion and the desire to positively impact others.
- Purpose isn't limited to one major goal; you can live purposefully in various areas of your life (e.g., as a storyteller, family member, friend, or professional).
- Life's significance comes not just from one big passion but from daily actions that add value to yourself and others.
- It's okay if you don't identify with a singular big purpose; you can still find joy and meaning in many activities.
- Continuously reflect on who you want to be and what you want from everyday situations. Being a good person is a meaningful purpose in itself.

3 PERSONAL EMPOWERMENT

How do you build confidence? Strength? Resilience? How do you become independent? Those are all things we will look at in this chapter.

✳ Building Self-Confidence, Resilience, and Independence

When you think about someone self-confident, you think of someone with swag, right? Like they walk into a room looking as confident as anything.

But *why* are they confident?

They aren't necessarily the best looking, smartest, most talented, kindest, or best at sports, but *they are happy being who they are* and that can be seen in every gesture they make.

Being confident *about* something is different. You become confident at reading after you've practiced enough to be able to read without any major struggles. But *having* self-confidence can mean you're totally cool about reading aloud even if you aren't the best reader. You're okay with who you are and where you are at with something, even if it's not at the top of a mountain (metaphorically speaking).

As mentioned in a previous chapter, just sitting down and contemplating what you're good at—from making your bed to being nice to people—can bring about a change in how you *feel* about yourself.

However, confidence comes from being alright with who you are and where you're at with things in your life.

I always say that true confidence brings about a sense of calm—you're okay with who you are, where you're at, and have an inner confidence that no matter what life throws at you, you'll be okay.

You'll find a lot of twenty-somethings who are cocky. They're going to change the world. They're going to get rich. They're going to excel at this or that. Maybe they've already proven they're excellent at something, made a bunch of money, or dated the hottest people in town.

The thing is, though, *that* kind of confidence isn't real confidence. Because when life happens, and it always does, they'll be shaken up pretty badly if they don't know how to deal with whatever happens to them. Life isn't just sports or business or being well-liked by friends.

Life keeps changing. Just when you've figured out how to do relationships, you get married and have to figure that out. Then you have kids, and what seemed so simple turns out to be a crazy ride.

Self-confidence comes in knowing you'll be okay no matter what life throws at you. You've accepted who you are and you're happy with it. That doesn't mean you aren't growing or learning; it simply means you aren't coming down on yourself because you don't have this or that talent or haven't yet learned this or that thing.

Some people lose track of who they are. They are propelled into a career with huge success and people see them as the rockstar or the businesswoman or the perfect mother. Only they wake a few years later and feel like they don't know themselves. Because they didn't stop to ask what else in life they wanted to explore. There's much more to them, but they don't know what it is.

If you can manage to stay confident knowing you don't have all the answers—you don't know how to behave on a date or at a job interview where things don't go as planned—if you can stay calm when things happen where you don't know what to do, then you're ahead of the game.

What many teens don't realize is that there is no magic number of when you turn into an adult and have all the answers. You keep learning and growing—at least if you want to. No matter how well you're dealing with life, there's always more to learn.

Resilience comes about when you get up after you fall down. To be able to get up, you have to stop judging yourself harshly, because that will leave you feeling defeated and you won't have the energy to get up. As Thomas Edison famously said, it wasn't a failure not to make a light bulb work in 100 experiments. He simply found out 100 ways *not* to make a light bulb. He didn't see it as failure; he saw it as progress.

As a teen, it can be difficult to feel okay after having lost something. You think that if you don't get into that particular school, or don't get that particular guy, it's the end of the line. Because nothing else can compare to those.

When you're forty, you realize there are a lot of schools that can teach you amazing things and where you can meet amazing people and have a great time. There are also a lot of guys. As Richard Branson, business magnate and owner of Virgin Atlantic Airways, said, "Businesses are like buses. If I missed one, there's another one coming." It's the same for most things in life.

No, no one opportunity will be like the one you just missed, but they could be greater.

Let's say you perform a choreography at an audition for a dance school. This is THE school. THE door opener you need to have a career as a dancer.

You don't get in—you failed the audition. You walk away devastated.

The following week, you have a performance at school. It's a silly little performance in comparison to the audition. There will be no famous choreographers in the audience this time. But you've decided you're going to become a dancer, so you still give it your all—you prepare well, and when you dance, it's as if you're transported to another place.

After the performance, a guy in the audience comes up to you. As it turns out, he's visiting his niece, but he runs a dance company in New York. He wants you to come train with his company.

You could have decided that if you didn't get into that one school, there would be no point in dancing anymore—especially not for an audience who doesn't know anything about dancing. But you didn't, because dancing is your life.

Defeats are usually temporary, so long as you have enough energy to get up and get going. You will have that energy if you don't get lost in thoughts of defeat. Those thoughts, on the other hand, will completely drain you.

Being right doesn't make you confident; *being curious* about what you can learn next does. It also makes you resilient. Instead of giving up when life hands you lemons, you just shrug your shoulders, try to learn from it, and move on.

This also has to do with not putting all your eggs in one basket. You can't build your happiness or confidence on just one thing. I've met more than one person who intended to have a career in sports only to have to change plans after injury.

Be curious about life and what's coming next, even if it's not the path you expected to go on.

There are also times when it's time to call it quits. If a company you launched is no longer making you money and you've tried everything to solve it, then it's time to quit before you start *losing* money.

Some of us have what it takes to dance on the big stage, others don't. You can still keep dancing and having fun, but you can't make a career out of it as a prima ballerina. You can be a dance teacher. Perhaps even a professor in dance. You can have a small dance company that performs at schools. You can have tons and tons of fun. So long as you're not still stuck at wanting to perform as a lead at the New York Ballet. Perhaps you will one day train and dance with them, though, as part of an educational initiative.

Life is filled with juicy stuff, even if it doesn't go according to the perfect plan. And sometimes that perfect plan has more to do with our ego than what we truly want.

Independence usually comes when we're self-confident enough to feel okay with being on our own in the big world. Again, that doesn't mean we have all the answers, it just means we're okay with not having them.

Independence is usually also linked to having the tools to deal with day-to-day life. If you don't know where to buy groceries, how to cook or order a meal, or how to pay your rent, you aren't ready for independence.

There will be a lot of things to learn when you leave home. You don't have to know them all up front, but you have to be willing to learn and take the initiative to do so.

KEY TAKEAWAYS

- Confidence grows through repeated practice until you master a skill.
- You can possess self-confidence without excelling in any area; it's about being content with who you are and where you are in life.
- Resilience develops when you don't take defeat personally, viewing it as a learning opportunity, which allows you to keep moving forward. Letting go of your ego helps you stay curious about what comes next rather than needing to succeed to feel good about yourself.
- Independence emerges when you feel confident enough to navigate life on your own, knowing how to find information as needed, even if you don't know everything.

✳ Making Great Decisions

We've all been there—or at least most of us have—in a space where we regret a decision we've made.

So how do you make great decisions?

There's no guide to life that teaches you how to make a decision, but there are some things most people would consider crucial when making decisions. And below you see one way of tackling decisions that will, hopefully, help you make great decisions!

1. **What's your goal?** What is it you want to get out of the situation once you've made your decision?
2. **What's important to you when it comes to this goal/decision?** Usually it's not just one thing that matters when making a decision, but several.
3. **Consider your values/guidelines for life.** What is important when it comes to this decision?
4. **Gather information.** The more you know, the better equipped you are for making a decision. Make sure your information comes

from reliable sources. If you ask others for information, consider whether they're biased or if they're just giving straight answers.

5. **List your options.** What options do you have? Weigh the pros and cons and consequences of each option. Remember to consider any potential risks. Also, ask yourself what it will feel like to be in the situation after making the decision.

6. **Consider your fears.** Are there options that frighten you, not because they're the wrong ones, but because if you choose them, you have to face a fear?

7. **Consider your bias or prejudices.** Are you avoiding a certain option because of prejudice as opposed to fact?

8. **Use your intuition.** Once you've gathered the information and written down your options, each with their own pros and cons, sit down and lean into your feelings about the options you're considering. Does anything feel right or wrong (and not because of fear or prejudice getting in the way)?

9. **Make a decision.** You have the facts, you have the different options, you've evaluated your own fears and prejudices in relation to each option, as well as the consequences, including any pros and cons. Take a few moments to breathe, then make your decision.

10. **Course correct.** If you learn it wasn't the best decision, course correct or perform damage control. We never know *everything* up front. We have to adjust as things happen. Plus, sometimes the worst mistakes turn out to be the best thing that could ever have happened as something really good comes out of it.

Let's do an example: so let's say you're choosing what college to attend.

1. **What's your goal (or goals)?**
   Getting a degree in engineering that is respected enough to open doors to internships and entry-level jobs.

2. **What's important to you when it comes to this goal/decision?**
   The school needs to be affordable or offer scholarships, be situated close to or in a town so I can find some part-time job easily, and I want the school to have some nice extracurricular activities on campus.

3. **Consider your values/guidelines for life.**
   I want a school that promotes learning in a fun and practical way, not just passing students through the system. I want the school to take pride in what it does.

4. **Gather information.**

   I've done online research and found ten schools that fit my criteria.

5. **List your options.**

   I've listed the ten schools and their pros and cons (expenses, closeness to a town, how nice the campus looks, the extracurricular programs they offer, how good their reputation is, etc.). I've closed my eyes and imagined being at each school and what life there would be like (and realized that in Connecticut the winters are a lot longer, colder, and darker, than here in Arizona!).

6. **Consider your fears.**

   While Harvard is expensive, it fits my criteria as it has an excellent scholarship program and everything else I want, but I'm scared the other students will be rich and arrogant.

7. **Consider your bias or prejudices.**

   I have a prejudice against the students at Harvard. Because one of my parents attended Syracuse, I feel drawn to attend that university, too. I have this idea that life in California is more fun, so I also feel drawn to California, but perhaps not for the reasons of studying.

8. **Use your intuition.**

   I've sat down, taken deep breaths, and thought through all the schools in my mind. Interestingly, I now feel like Harvard might be the best option if I get accepted and get a scholarship, followed by the California Institute of Technology.

9. **Make a decision.**

   I'm going to apply to all ten schools, but I have listed them in my order of preference, so if I get accepted to more than one, I know what to choose, though if more information comes to light, I'll also consider reordering my list.

10. **Course correct.**

    If things really don't feel right after I get accepted somewhere (beyond the first few weeks, that might be really hard as I'm still getting used to everything and making new friends), I know I can apply for a transfer.

Some decisions we make almost without thinking. We're on autopilot, or we use our feelings to guide us. But feelings can lie. And it's never more apparent than when we have a crush on someone … who turns out not to be so nice when we get to know them. But if there's one thing that can blind us to that, it's attraction.

I'll talk more about attraction and how to make good choices when it comes to crushes later, but remember to always ask yourself what you want out of the situation. A boyfriend shouldn't just make you feel a bit giddy. He would have to contribute something of value to a relationship. A school isn't just cool because Martin Scorsese, an award-winning film director, went there (and now you know how I first went about picking colleges), but because it offers a solid program where you learn the skills you need to succeed in your chosen field. The food we eat isn't just good because it tastes good—it needs to nourish us.

When you are about to make a decision—stop. Take a moment to check you aren't in a heightened emotional state. Then, go over the list. After that, make a decision.

It's never wise to make decisions when you're over the moon or down in the dumps. You aren't thinking clearly at that moment. Take a few minutes to breathe. You should always do that before making decisions, if nothing else.

KEY TAKEAWAYS

- There's no definitive expert guide for making decisions, but we can ask ourselves key questions to navigate the process effectively.
- It's important to consider our own wants, fears, biases, and prejudices alongside the facts. Visualizing the outcomes of our decisions can help us understand what we might truly feel.
- Avoid making decisions when you're extremely happy or feeling down. If you must decide during these times, practice a mindfulness exercise to calm yourself beforehand.

✳ Coping with Stress and Anxiety

We have already tackled this topic in the sections about managing our emotions, so I'll keep this brief, but I want to bring attention to it, because it's important. None of us function properly when we are stressed or anxious and there's so much you can do to calm down and get happy, so it's important you're aware of that.

We all have slightly different stressors and accompanying dysfunctional patterns. For example, when I have so many things to do, I don't know where to start. And while doing one thing, I might very well be getting stressed about another thing that needs to get done. That leads to poor focus and a burst of stress hormones that do more harm than good.

As a result, I now tell myself that the best course of action is to forget about everything else and just do that one thing. It doesn't help thinking about any of the other items on the to-do list—the fastest way to get through it is to focus on one thing at a time.

I also find that doing breathing exercises can quickly help me step out of brain fog and into focus if I do end up feeling overwhelmed. It also helps me when I get emotional about things.

Because I do these exercises, I have better focus, get more done, and am less stressed. I also do my best to get exercise, as otherwise I feel sluggish and work slower.

We are all different, and some of us get stressed or anxious faster than others and for different reasons. You might get stressed in social situations, when presented with a test, or when dating.

When you get triggered, remind yourself of what's working in your life (there's more to your life than what's just triggered you), go somewhere you feel safe, and take a moment to breathe. If you can, also envision something that makes you feel calm and safe.

You can also try out various other techniques to calm the stress and anxiety. Read books about how other people deal with their stressors or look up exercises online, just be sure they come from verified sources. For example, Healthline publishes articles reviewed by medical professionals, but that GIF on Facebook saying that drinking super-sweet carbonated soda will calm you down probably isn't correct.

Make sure to incorporate the mood boosters in your daily routine as they will help your mind stay happy and healthy to start with. And that, in and of itself, means you're less likely to become stressed and anxious.

If you find yourself stressed and anxious often, or the stress or anxiety is intense (such as having panic attacks), seek professional help. You don't have to deal with it alone. And you don't have to keep suffering—there are so many techniques that can help you overcome both stress and anxiety.

KEY TAKEAWAYS

If you feel stressed, or anxious, try to go to a place where you feel safe and spend a few minutes doing mindfulness exercises. If you're still stressed or anxious by the end of the day, meditate.

If you find yourself more stressed or anxious than you would like, especially if it interferes with your normal daily activities and/or lasts longer than two weeks, speak with someone. It can help to talk to a loved one, but you might also need a professional to give you the tools you need to flourish.

✳ Overcoming Adversity and Seeking Support and Resources

The one thing you can be sure about in life is that you will encounter adversity. Things will happen that are difficult, upsetting, and sad. You will also hit bumps in the road on your way to your goals. So how do you overcome adversity?

Overcoming adversity is similar to building resilience, but here are some questions to ask yourself when you feel like giving up:

- What story are you telling yourself about what happened? Are you seeing what happened in a helpful way, or are you putting yourself down?
- Can you seek help from someone who has experience in this area?
- Have you approached the situation from the wrong angle? How can you course correct?
- Is this what you really want, or is your goal attached to what others say you should achieve?

Of course, there are different forms of adversity. Losing a game is different from losing a friend. How we see things and the stories we tell ourselves about what happened matter.

Losing someone, whether through going separate ways or death, is difficult. But you can find ways of moving forward by feeling gratitude for the time spent together, seeing what you've learned, and focusing on what you want to experience next. It's also important you start participating in things that bring meaning to your life in the present moment, even if, at first, showing up is hard and you don't get any immediate joy out of it.

Similarly, losing a job or something important can be really distressing. Again, there are ways of looking at the situation that can help you move forward. And it's really important we learn to do that if we want the most out of life.

For example, after a relationship falls apart, it's easy to think you'll never find love again. But are all men like the guy you dated? No. Are there people out there having great relationships? Yes. Could you have great relationships? Probably. You might need to learn more about picking the right partner and communicating better, but yes, you could have a great relationship with someone.

We are always making things up about ourselves, others, and life at large. And what we make up dictates, not just how we act in the moment, but who we become.

And the funny thing is, once we've made up our mind about things, we tend to act in such a way that we confirm our own beliefs.

For example, if you've had bad experiences with teachers, you might start thinking that all teachers are unfair. When you meet a good teacher, you might act coldly toward them, which might fuel them to act in such a way that you prove your point. The same holds true for relationships—if you expect someone to hurt you, you might push them away.

Remember that when things go wrong, when someone is mean, or when life doesn't turn out the way you expected, you have to stop and ask yourself what story you're telling and how you can rewrite it. This way, you can use the event to fuel you to lead a better and happier life.

When things go wrong, it's also important to remember the mood boosters in chapter 1. Eating well, exercising, getting enough sleep at regular hours, and various mindfulness exercises can help us stay emotionally stable during rough times.

There's another thing to remember when the tough times hit: our friends, family, and professional support network.

Friends are there to help, whether it's offering advice, a shoulder to cry on, or practical support. Having people around you who care makes a huge difference.

There are other forms of support we sometimes need—therapists, coaches, or mentors who can help us navigate challenges. You don't have to do everything on your own.

Before I wrap this up, there's one thing you need to be aware of: Just as there's always going to be rain, there's always going to be adversity. Plan for it. Life is not a perfect ride. It's a ride filled with ups and downs. And when the downs hit, you want to have tools to deal with them. You want that support network. You want the professionals you can call. You want to be able to rewrite the story so that you empower yourself to dust yourself off and move towards better things.

You can't avoid pain, but you can avoid getting stuck wallowing in it with the right tools, people, and a dash of love for yourself, others, and life. Because you need to remember that love when the bad times come calling. It also helps having faith—believing in a better tomorrow and actively working towards it.

KEY TAKEAWAYS

- Storms and sunshine are both inevitable parts of life.
- Remember the sunshine during tough times and prepare your toolkit for dealing with storms.
- Having a supportive network of friends and family, or a support group, is crucial for navigating challenges.
- If you struggle to find a positive perspective or feel overwhelmed, seek professional help. Therapists can assist with rebuilding confidence and understanding relationships.
- Surround yourself with friends and relatives who uplift you and remind you of your worth.
- Be mindful of the stories you tell yourself, as they can either lead to defeat or empower you to overcome adversity and emerge stronger and happier.

✳ Stand Up for Yourself

Just as there will be adversity in our lives, there will be times when we need to stand up for ourselves.

No one should ever treat you with disrespect.

No one should ever make you do things against your wishes.

If this happens, you have to stand up and say no. Then calmly explain what it is you want.

The funny thing is, when we ask for what we want, we often get it.

But if we get angry and start screaming at people, we back away and hide in a corner, or we try to manipulate people, we often don't get it.

If you feel you're in a situation where you can't ask for what you want as it's too hostile an environment, then you have to ask for outside assistance.

Remember as well that sometimes people disrespect you, not because it's their intention, but because they don't know better, or misunderstood something. So remain calm and spell out what the issue is and how you'd like things to be resolved.

There are times in my life when I've done something wrong. We all do. But those of us who care do our best to make amends.

It's so important to ask people for what you want. The good ones will hear you out, and if what you're saying is reasonable, they'll do their best to change their ways.

The thing is, sometimes we don't even know what we want. And that's when we follow the crowd. If someone suggests something, we go along with it, even though in the back of our mind, there's a niggling feeling that something isn't right. That's when you have to stop and ask yourself, "Is this really what I want?" And if it isn't, you have to say so.

It's not always easy to have the guts to tell your truth, but it's important you do so. The exercise I mentioned where you think through an event before it happens can help you out. So can relaxation exercises. Imagine yourself completely relaxed delivering your message.

Sometimes we fear what we will lose if we speak up. "Will my boyfriend dump me if I say how I see this situation?" Perhaps he will. But how will you feel twenty years from now if you keep living a life that doesn't make you happy?

At times, it can be wise to wait to speak up if it's about a job and you don't have a second one lined up, for example. However, you have to learn to speak your truth if you want to live your dream life. Because if you don't, you're never going to get to that dream life. You'll simply accept what's given to you and not demand more.

If someone suggests a date you're not comfortable with, a task at work you're not comfortable with, or says or does something to you that offends you, you have got to speak up. And if you do it respectfully, without making assumptions about the other person, chances are things will work out if the person you're dealing with is a decent person.

If they aren't a decent person, if they laugh and make fun of your requests, well, then they've proven they aren't someone whom you want in your life. And sometimes we have to lose what we don't want to find what we do want. But by speaking out, we also have the opportunity to fix things, if they are fixable.

Always remember how you want to see yourself and don't let yourself be dictated by other people's opinions.

KEY TAKEAWAYS

- To achieve what you want in life, you must ask for it.
- Stand up for yourself and say no if someone treats you poorly or asks you to do something you're uncomfortable with.
- Avoid making assumptions about other people's motives; instead, ask for what you want politely.
- Have these conversations when you're calm, rather than in a heated moment.
- If you're nervous, practice mentally preparing to express yourself clearly and confidently.
- Remember that speaking up gives others the chance to help fix things; if they're unwilling, something better is waiting for you.
- If you're unhappy at a job, consider applying for new positions before addressing your concerns to minimize risk.
- If you're in a hostile or dangerous situation, prioritize your safety and seek external assistance immediately.

4 EXPRESS YOURSELF—FINDING YOUR VOICE

Finding your voice and making yourself heard is easy-peasy ... or not. We all have different ways of communicating and sometimes it requires ... translation. Some people seem to find it so easy to communicate, while others struggle immensely. So let's dive into this to figure out how you can find your voice and use it!

✳ Self-Expression and Creativity

Self-expression can be a lot of fun, and there are tons of ways to express yourself that you might not even realize. Below are a few ideas:

- o **Painting or sculpting:** This can just be color blobs and abstract things that communicate how you're feeling.
- o **Acting in theater:** Express different parts of yourself. Create monologues and even plays that you act out.
- o **Building things:** Create pieces that represent how you feel or what you're dreaming about.
- o **Journaling:** You don't even have to write full pieces; just jot down a list of words to describe how you're feeling right now.
- o **Writing stories:** Sometimes writing about other people frees us up as it doesn't feel as personal (even if it is).
- o **Creating a new wardrobe/look:** Dress up at home to express something. You can even make your own clothes or go to a charity shop to find clothes that match how you feel.
- o **Making a vision board:** Cut out pictures to represent what you dream about for the future.

- ○ **Making music:** Whether you play an instrument or sing, you can express a lot.
- ○ **Making a movie with your phone:** You can make movies with your phone and edit them with various apps.
- ○ **Coding:** Come up with an app or program that shows how you see the world.
- ○ **Cooking:** Put your feelings on display through your cooking.
- ○ **Starting a business:** You can set up a business where the products are an expression of something you believe in.

There are a myriad of ways to express your thoughts and feelings through creative adventures, and this list is nowhere near complete.

Have a think about what hobbies you'd like to try to express yourself.

Why is self-expression important?

It can help you come to terms with your emotions. It can also be a place where you enhance your creativity, build a brand, or simply build a stronger voice. By challenging yourself, you become more confident.

There is one thing you need to remember when it comes to creative self-expression: there's a difference between expressing yourself for the sake of self-expression and for effective communication. Making a movie that explores our emotions is one thing; making a movie other people understand is another. More about effective communication in the next section.

It's healthy to express ourselves in ways we enjoy. It can help us let go of emotions or indulge in the emotions we enjoy.

If we get stuck painting only sad themes, on the other hand, it's perhaps time to seek help, or move on to expressing something else.

A couple of years ago, I started writing poetry on a more frequent basis after years of not doing it. I then made a decision that I'd only write about the things that made me happy.

Why? Because I didn't want to revel in unpleasantness. I wanted to be inspired. I wanted to write about the things that put a smile on my face and made me feel alive. I wanted true passion and not anger and frustration to fuel my writing.

When I'm upset, on the other hand, it can be useful to write down my thoughts as I work through them. I can more clearly see the situation and come up with solutions or find ways to move forward if I'm sad.

Once I've come to terms with something, I can move on to finding the things I love and get excited about and put that excitement down in a poem.

Also, remember to play and have fun. Never mind finding your voice or expressing yourself if that sounds daunting. There are times when you just need to do what you love for no other reason than that you love it. It's not to build a career, improve your skills, or communicate your truth. It's just for fun. But while having fun, you often find your voice!

Hobbies are things we might take for granted as kids if we have access to extracurricular activities, but as we enter adulthood, they often fall to the wayside. Work, friends, life—there's just so much to do. But having hobbies can help us destress, build connections, and get through rough patches in life. It's super important to find things to do that you love that aren't tied to your work or family.

KEY TAKEAWAYS

- Communicating can serve different purposes: telling a story, being understood, entertaining, or simply expressing yourself.
- Experimenting with various forms of expression can enhance creativity and provide an emotional outlet.
- Self-expression doesn't have to be complex; simple activities like painting or building can be fulfilling.
- Hobbies, whether creative or not, are essential for living our passions, reducing stress, and having fun.
- During tough times, hobbies can help us regain strength and rekindle our desire for life, grounding us in the process.

❋ Effective Communication

As mentioned, there's a difference between self-expression and effective communication.

When we express ourselves for the sake of expressing ourselves, we are simply working through our own thoughts and feelings. It's for our own sake.

Expressing ourselves so that other people understand us is a bit of a science.

- Be clear. Don't hint. Don't insinuate. Spell it out.
- Use your body language to emphasize your words. If you say something powerful, act powerfully. If you want to let someone into your confidence, open yourself up to them.
- Don't assume you know what the other person is thinking, so always approach people with respect (as a human) and give them the benefit of the doubt (as to what you believe they're thinking or what their intentions are).

Effective communication is always clear.

"I kinda miss you" versus "I'd love to spend more time with you. I know your schedule's changed but how about we make a plan to set aside two hours every week where we get to be alone. Not with friends, not watching a movie, but doing something together where we truly enjoy each other's company."

"You're annoying. I don't like you" versus "It really annoys me when you disrupt me every five minutes when I'm playing games online with my friends. I'd rather you leave me alone now, so I have time later to play with you. Would that work for you? I can even set an alarm and when that goes off, I'll stop playing video games and play with you."

It's so easy to yell "I hate you" in the heat of the moment when your sibling has annoyed you. But what you truly mean is that you hate whatever it is *they're doing* and you'd really love for them to do something else so that the two of you can get along.

We also sometimes forget why people are doing what they're doing. Is it to get our attention (even if it's in the wrong way)? Is it because they're feeling sad or upset? Is it because they're bored? Is it because they're jealous?

To create great relationships, we have to ask questions and we need to be clear when we express what we want.

But what should you do if someone is angry with you about something?

What we normally do is defend ourselves, shrink away, or go on the offensive (attack)—saying the nastiest thing we can think of and spending the next month regretting it. Sometimes we even manage to say something so hurtful that our relationship with a person falls apart.

So what should we do if someone is angry with us?

Listen. Acknowledge it. Get to the root of it. Solve it.

"I hear you're upset right now. If I understand you correctly, you're upset that I missed our date last night?" If they confirm that's the case, apologize if you're at fault and tell them what you'll do to make up for it, or explain why they got the wrong end of the stick if they are mistaken.

If you feel hurt by their attitude, first, try to figure out what's bothering them and solve that. Then calmly explain that how they approached it hurt your feelings. "I understand you're upset that I missed the date. However, I feel hurt that you don't know me well enough to understand there was a valid reason for it. I really care about you and wouldn't hurt you on purpose."

Can you see how approaching it that way is a lot better than starting to yell at them, or just walking away?

"Is it helpful, is it kind, is it necessary?" is a great thing to ask yourself before you speak. If someone is angry and rude, don't sink to their level. Act as the person you're proud to be.

When we speak with people, it's also important to be polite and to show you care. Ask them about their day. How they are doing. Wish them a good evening. And be sincere.

Consider "Hey, Mom, I want you to pick me up at five" versus "Hey, Mom, I hope you're having a good day. How's work going? Can you please pick me up at five? Thank you! Hugs."

If you love your mom, if you're curious about how her day is going, if you want her to have a great day, express it. Don't just assume she knows. She doesn't. She might know you love her, but she needs to hear it to feel it. We will speak about this in an upcoming chapter about relationships, but after you've read about the five love languages, revisit this section. Do you know your parents' and siblings' love languages? Do they know yours? Just because you're family doesn't mean you don't need to work on your relationships—you do.

Caring about someone also means we listen. When someone speaks, look at them. What are they communicating with their facial expressions and body language at large? What are they saying? Truly saying? And don't just try to mindread—ask questions.

Most of us are busy analyzing, coming up with solutions, judging them, or thinking about how what someone is saying relates to our own life. As a result, we aren't really present to them.

Some time ago, the idea of active listening was developed as a response to this tendency. The ability to be present and simply listen.

Unless you take in what the other person is saying and read the clues in their body language, you have no idea how to answer them. You're just moving the conversation in the direction you have in mind.

KEY TAKEAWAYS

- Always be clear in communication; the way you phrase things can drastically change the response you receive.
- Adding context and emotion to your statements helps the other person understand your feelings better.
- When someone is angry, instead of reacting, make sure they feel heard. Clarify their concerns before explaining your side.
- Upset people often just need to feel listened to. Once you understand their perspective, you can calmly address the issue.
- Politeness goes a long way in conversation—showing care and curiosity can open people up.
- The key to a great conversation is not just talking but listening without judgment, being fully present in the moment.

5 BODY POSITIVITY

When we hit our teens, our bodies change. We grow breasts. We get our periods. Hair starts sprouting out of every pore (or at least that's what it feels like). Pimples pop up. We might have a sudden growth spurt. Everything's changing, so how do you embrace your new self and take care of your body? And deal with the big P (your period)?

✳ How Our Bodies Change During Puberty

During puberty, our bodies change. A lot. And while some of it is really cool, it can also be frightening, or simply feel weird. Like hair under your armpits!

It's a natural part of growing up. You're turning into a woman! Soon you'll be living life on your own terms. But don't fret—you will have the time you need to find your feet.

Growth Spurt

One of the first things you might notice is getting taller. This can happen quickly, so don't be surprised if your clothes suddenly feel too small!

Body Shape

Your hips will widen, and you might gain weight around your thighs and chest. This is all part of developing a more mature figure. Just remember we're all different—whether you're a slim ballerina or femme fatale with swaying hips, it's just as perfect. Find women with your body type who inspire you instead of comparing yourself to others. Thanks to the online world, there are plenty of role models out there in all shapes and sizes.

Breasts

Breast development is one of the earliest signs of puberty. It starts with a small lump under each nipple that grows over time. It's normal for one breast to develop before the other and for them to be a bit sore. They can also become sore just before your period every month. If it gets incredibly painful though, seek medical advice.

When your breasts start growing, start bra shopping. A bralette or triangle bra without metal wiring is a good place to start. Once your breasts get a bit bigger, using a bra with more support might be better—you have to experiment to find what works for you.

Remember, everyone's breasts look different. Some women have big nipples, some small; some have round breasts, others oval. Media often shows unrealistic images of breasts, but in reality, they come in all shapes and sizes.

Hair Growth

Darker, coarser hair will start growing around your pubic area and under your arms. Fine hair might also appear on your legs or near your belly button.

Some women choose to shave or wax their legs and/or armpits, others don't. As you grow older, you might also want to wax parts of your pubic area. Many women do a bikini wax, meaning they wax so that when wearing a bikini, no hair sticks out. Some women prefer to shave, but in the bikini area, it's easy to get ingrown hairs or a rash from shaving, which is why many stick with waxing (even if it's painful!). If you shave, be sure to use gentle moisturizers (no alcohol) before and after to prevent a rash.

Some women prefer using hair removal creams to shaving and waxing. Just beware as they do contain chemicals.

Some people also wax or shave their arms, but know that if you do, the hair might not grow back looking as uniform as it does now.

Each method has pros and cons and going natural is also fine—you do you. Remember, there's no right or wrong choice here; it's about what makes you feel comfortable and confident.

Skin Changes

Hormonal changes can lead to acne breakouts, and due to genetics, some people may also be more prone to acne in the first place. It can be really, really irritating. And sure enough, every time you have a big event, party, or date coming up, you get a pimple square on your nose! Or you suffer from permanent skin trouble, which is even more irritating and can make you feel unattractive. Thankfully, there are ways to manage it:

- **Eat a healthy diet:** A balanced (i.e. you get your carbs, proteins, and fats), mainly whole foods, diet filled with vegetables and very little sugar or processed foods tends to work wonders. A healthy diet also helps prevent inflammation.
- **Stay hydrated:** Your skin needs water.
- **Get the right skincare products:** Avoid using a harsh soap that will deplete your skin of oils, causing it to produce more oil. Consult a dermatologist for recommendations or experiment with acne products carefully. Always do a patch test before trying out new products to avoid irritation.

If you suffer from bad skin, look up tips online from dermatologists on how to manage it, but always double check your sources. Just because one person recommends something doesn't mean it's good.

Lastly, if you can't manage to get your skin under control, see a dermatologist. In severe cases, you might need antibiotics. Some people also find success with herbal infusions or essential oils, but you need to do your own research first and ask a professional for advice before you try it.

Hygiene

You might sweat more in your teens because your sweat glands become more active in puberty, so washing your armpits and feet daily becomes important. You don't need to use soap all over your body when washing, but do use soap for your armpits unless you naturally smell amazing.

Choose deodorants and body lotions that don't have harsh chemicals as they can irritate your skin. Find brands that use ingredients that you don't mind sinking into your skin (as your skin sort of "eats" what's put on it)—do your research online and always double check the source.

Washing your genitals (NOT inside your vagina) with plain water or soap *specifically designed for that purpose* (though many experts caution against any form of soap) once or twice a day is also important. Regular soap will irritate your lady parts, and the odds are you'll develop fungal (yeast) infections caused by candida or bacterial infections called bacterial vaginosis. These conditions can be itchy and uncomfortable but are treatable. Candida can be treated with over-the-counter medications, but might need medical attention if it gets severe, while bacterial vaginosis will need treatment from a doctor with prescription meds.

These infections can occur even if you do not wash yourself with soap. Anything that disrupts the healthy bacteria in your vagina can cause them, such as using sanitary products during your period.

Some ways to maintain vaginal health:

- Eat a balanced diet and consider taking probiotics for good bacteria.
- Use natural moisturizers during your period (and at other times if needed) to prevent dryness. You can try coconut oil if you're not allergic to it.
- Avoid douching—your vagina cleans itself.

Discharge

During your teens, or even earlier, you'll notice you'll start getting vaginal discharge. This is totally normal and will become thicker when you ovulate (more about that in the section about periods).

Discharge is kind of like your vagina's own moisturizer, and you need it for a happy and healthy vagina. If you suddenly have what seems like too much discharge, or it gets smelly, you should see a doctor—it can be a sign of infection.

Periods

During puberty, you'll get your first period. This is when the lining of your uterus sheds and leaves your body through your vagina. You'll likely see blood on your underwear. Periods can be irregular for the first few years, and that's totally normal. More about your period in the next section as it deserves a whole section to explain it properly!

UTIs

Urinary tract infections (UTIs) are not part of puberty, thank goodness, but as a woman, you should know what they are because they are common. They can occur after having sexual intercourse, may be caused by drinking too little water or too much alcohol, having a cold, or getting a vaginal infection of some kind. None of those things necessarily lead to UTIs, they can simply make UTIs more likely.

Drinking lots of water, drinking cranberry juice (preferably one with very little sugar added as bacteria feeds off sugar), going to the bathroom to urinate when you need to, and taking probiotics might be helpful in preventing UTIs. You should also always wipe from front to back when using the toilet, as bacteria from your anus can otherwise travel up your urethra and cause an infection. If you get a bad case of UTI, it hurts. A lot. And you should seek medical attention.

Does all of this sound like a bore? Or overwhelming? At first it might appear that way, but with time, you'll come to love your adult body. Just be patient with yourself as you're going through the changes. It happens at different paces for everyone. If you have any questions or concerns, talk to a parent, doctor, or trusted adult. They can help you understand what's happening and navigate this exciting time!

KEY TAKEAWAYS

As you reach puberty you can expect:

- A growth spurt
- Wider hips and potential weight gain around the thighs and hips
- The development of breasts
- More body hair, including pubic hair and hair under your armpits
- Getting your period
- Hormonal changes which can cause acne
- A change in the way you smell—hygiene and daily washing becomes important
- Vaginal discharge
- A greater potential of UTIs

Leading a healthy lifestyle—eating and sleeping well, as well as exercising—and spending time with people who support you is important for you to stay on top of your mental health as you navigate this time. If something is particularly bothering you, speak with someone about it.

✳ The Period

The big P.

I don't think anyone will tell you that having your period is a lovely experience, bodily speaking. It often hurts. It can make you tired, angry, sad, and irritated. And there's always that "lovely" feeling of waking up and realizing you started bleeding during the night.

BUT having your period is part of entering womanhood. It's part of the cycle that allows you to have children, if you want them. It's part of being a woman, and it should be cherished as such.

Most girls get their period between the ages of 10–15, but some may start earlier or later. If you haven't gotten yours by age 16 or two years after your breasts started developing, see a gynecologist.

Usually, you get your period within two years after breasts start to develop. You also tend to experience vaginal discharge (i.e. mucus that keeps your vagina lubricated) six to twelve months beforehand.

To better understand what's happening during your cycle, let's look at what's going on in your body.

Ovaries: Store and release eggs.

Follicles: Sacs that store eggs.

Corpus luteum: The empty follicle left behind after ovulation (when the egg leaves).

Fallopian tubes: Transport eggs from the ovaries to the uterus.

Uterus: Where a fertilized egg implants and grows into a baby.

Vagina: The birth canal that leads out of the uterus to the exterior of the body.

Phase 1: Fresh Start (Follicular Phase)

- This phase kicks things off right after your period ends. It's like your body is hitting the reset button and getting ready for a new cycle.
- Inside your ovaries, an egg chills out in a follicle. This follicle starts to grow and mature, just like an egg getting ready to hatch.
- As the follicle grows bigger, your body releases estrogen. This hormone is like a friendly message to the lining of your uterus

(where a fertilized egg would implant) telling it to thicken up and get comfy. Imagine it like preparing a cozy nest for a potential guest.

Phase 2: Ovulation

- This is the halfway point of the cycle and kind of like the main event! The strongest follicle releases the egg into your fallopian tube. It's like the egg is finally graduating and ready for the next stage.
- This usually happens around the middle of your cycle, but it can vary a bit from month to month. You might experience some mid-cycle cramping or twinges around your ovaries during ovulation. This is just your body doing its thing.
- This is when you're fertile, meaning you can get pregnant.

Phase 3: Waiting Game (Luteal Phase)

- The empty follicle left behind by the egg transforms into a corpus luteum. This little guy releases progesterone, another hormone that keeps the lining of your uterus nice and thick, just in case the egg gets fertilized. Think of it like maintaining a cozy nest in case the egg becomes fertilized and you need a place for a baby to grow. (So at this stage, you're still fertile.)
- If there's no fertilization, the corpus luteum gets the message and stops producing progesterone, signaling to your body that it can shed the egg and the nest.
- This drop in progesterone can lead to a bunch of not-so-fun symptoms called premenstrual syndrome (PMS). You might experience cramps, bloating, mood swings, headaches, or breast tenderness. It's like your body is bummed there's no visitor and is starting to clean up for next time.
- To help prevent PMS, you can check out the mood boosters in a previous chapter, as they can help keep your hormones stable. You can also try various herbs, but do so with the help of a specialist. Lastly, if it's really bad (and some people get it really bad), see a doctor.
- Note that if you get really bad PMS, it's called premenstrual dysphoric disorder (PDDM) and usually occurs seven to 10 days before your period, while PMS usually happens within five days of your period. If you think you have PDDM, seek medical help.

Phase 4: Shedding Time (Menstruation)

- Remember that comfy nest lining? Since there's no fertilized egg (no visitor!), it's not needed anymore. So, your body sheds the lining along with some blood. This is your period! It usually lasts for 3–7 days.
- When you have your period, your uterus is cramping to get rid of the lining. These cramps are what pushes the blood out of your body. And these cramps are what can cause pain if they are severe. You might also feel incredibly tired, experience brain fog, get a headache, have to use the bathroom frequently (to poop, sorry, ladies), or even feel a bit dizzy. Depending on the severity, you might have to spend a day at home. Over-the-counter pain relievers (ibuprofen is often recommended, but cannot be taken on an empty stomach as it can cause ulcers and always check with your doctor if you have a condition or take other meds) are enough to help most women keep going as normal, but everyone's different.

Your period is your body's way of saying, "Nope, no pregnancy this month. Let's clean up and get ready for the next chance!"

Your cycle might not be exactly 28 days like some sources say. It can take a while to settle into a regular pattern, and that's completely normal. For example, maybe one month your cycle will be 18 days, the next 30. I remember having my period every two weeks!

What helps these days with tracking your period? Apps!

There can also be signs when your period is coming (for example, some women feel ovulation each month). You can experience spotting and cramping, some get a headache just before their period, or extreme mood swings, and if you track those, the app will tell you when to expect your period even if it's not regular.

If you ever stop getting your period, it suddenly becomes super irregular, or it never settles into a fairly regular pattern, see a gynecologist as there are many different reasons this could happen (ranging from stress or depression to harmless cysts that may need removing). As a teen, it's also good to simply see a gynecologist for a regular checkup simply to see everything is okay. Be sure to pick a female gynecologist if seeing a man would make you feel uneasy.

Just as cycle length varies from woman to woman, so does the amount of blood loss you experience during your period. Most women lose between 2–3 tablespoons in total, though it often seems like a lot more!

Some women experience heavier periods, but if you experience any of the below, you should seek medical help:

- Bleed for more than seven days
- Have to change a tampon or pad after only two hours (and not just once, but several times)
- Need to change pads during the night (even though you use the jumbo size ones) as it bleeds through
- Have blood clots the size of a quarter or larger

Also, if you have constant pain for several days in a row, so intense pain you feel like you can't handle it, not even after taking pain killers, even if the pain only lasts for a day, or you feel super fatigued, or you get super emotional for days on end, you need to seek medical advice.

Likewise, if you get very emotional (super sensitive, angry, and/or depressed) for about a week mid-cycle every month, seek medical help as you might have PDDM.

PMS is different as it happens in the days leading up to your period. While it can involve physical things like headaches, bloating, and aching breasts, I've found that my mood is one of the worst (and, sometimes, funniest) aspects. One time, my boss handed me an Excel sheet to fill in, and I had to hide my tears as I got so upset. While I do hate Excel sheets, I couldn't see why it should set me off crying … until I realized I was likely to get my period soon! Sure enough, within hours, I got my period.

Another time, I was sitting on my couch, relaxing and then, suddenly, I started feeling really depressed about my life. Just like that. As I was observing my own thoughts, I was gobsmacked—what was going on? Again, I realized my period was coming.

Looking back, these events can be amusing, but they can also be really difficult to handle. The night before my period, I often get tired and I still have to care for my kids. If they're being difficult, I find it hard to reign in my emotions. I get angry. I get sad. And while I'd like to be left alone so no one suffers from my bad mood and emotional state, I can't do that. The kids still need me. So I have to do my best to remember it's just my hormones and stop myself from reacting to whatever is going on.

While it can feel unsettling at first, there's no point fighting your period. You will have it. Embracing it and thinking of it as part of the initiation to womanhood is a much better approach. It makes you feel feminine and empowered, as opposed to irritated with "the mess" that's your period.

Speaking of mess—it's important to wash yourself with water morning and night when you have your period to avoid it getting smelly. (Never ever wash inside your vagina, and never use regular soap on your lady parts!)

Another thing to bear in mind is to always have a "period kit" with you. That includes pads or whatever you use when having your period, a change of underwear, and painkillers if you tend to get pain.

Now let's look at products that you can use for your period.

Disposable Products

- **Pads:** These are adhesive strips that stick to your underwear and absorb menstrual blood. They come in various lengths, thicknesses, and absorbances for different flow levels.
- **Tampons:** These are absorbent tubes inserted into the vagina to collect menstrual blood. They come in various absorbencies and with or without applicators for easier (or harder, depending on how you feel about applicators) insertion.
- **Pantyliners:** These are thin liners worn in underwear for light discharge or backup protection.

Even if you use a tampon or a menstrual cup, it can be good to use a pantyliner just in case there are any leaks.

It's important you learn how heavy your flow is so that you can change these products as and when needed. Furthermore, you should NEVER use the same tampon for more than eight hours, nor should you use tampons while sleeping. Tampons can cause toxic shock syndrome (though it's incredibly rare), which can lead to sepsis (an extreme reaction to infection), which in the worst scenario can lead to death. This is why it's essential to change tampons often and never use them at night.

This is what the FDA in 2024 says: "**Know the signs of toxic shock syndrome (TSS) and how to reduce your risk.** Symptoms and signs of TSS may include a sudden fever (usually 102°F or more), vomiting, diarrhea, fainting or feeling like you are going to faint when standing up, dizziness, or a rash that looks like a sunburn. If you have any of these symptoms during your period or soon after your period, stop using tampons and seek medical attention immediately."

Also, remember what I said about coconut oil? If you are sensitive, using a lubricant can help prevent a lot of discomfort and the potential of developing a yeast infection when using sanitary products. Of course, there are other lubricants than coconut oil and you need to find what works for you. You should NOT use coconut oil if you are allergic to coconut! And be sure to use a clean spoon or similar to scoop it out as you don't want bacteria to get into the coconut oil before applying it. You can apply it to your vagina, to your pads, or to your tampons. It depends on where you get dry.

Reusable Products

- **Menstrual cups:** These are flexible silicone cups inserted into the vagina to collect menstrual blood. They can be reused for several cycles after being sterilized.
- **Period underwear:** This is specially designed underwear with built-in absorbent layers to collect menstrual blood. They are reusable and washable.
- **Period discs:** These are similar to menstrual cups but sit higher in the vagina, collecting menstrual blood. They are also reusable.

Again, remember to change these as and when needed. A menstrual cup should be changed at least every 12 hours and should never be reused without first being cleaned with water or a disinfectant that does NOT destroy neither the cup nor your vagina (no alcohol, no essential oils). There are special disinfectants for this purpose. You can always rinse the disinfectant off with water in case you don't want any residue. After each period, the cup should be disinfected, usually boiled. You can have a special pot for this purpose.

Menstrual cups sometimes move a bit higher up than where you inserted them and should they be difficult to get out, try pushing (as if you were to give birth!). You will also find instructions online from menstrual cup providers on how best to remove them if they feel a bit "stuck." Worst-case scenario, see a doctor to remove it, though the chances you'll ever need that are very slim!

Additional Products

- **Pain relievers:** Over-the-counter pain relievers like ibuprofen or acetaminophen can help with cramps. Just remember to follow the instructions. For example, ibuprofen requires that you eat something before you take the pills as it can cause stomach discomfort or even bleeding otherwise. Sometimes you don't need painkillers—a walk can help enough (often moving is preferable to lying down).
- **Heating pad or hot water bottle:** Applying heat to your lower abdomen can help relieve cramps. A hot bath might also help.
- **Wipes:** These can be used for cleaning during your period. Choose fragrance-free wipes for sensitive skin.
- **Leakproof underwear:** These can be worn for additional security and peace of mind, especially when using tampons or cups.

Choosing the right product depends on several factors:

- Your personal preference and comfort level.
- Heaviness of your flow.
- Your lifestyle and activities.

If you experience any discomfort or have questions, talk to a parent, doctor, or trusted adult. It will also help to educate yourself. Look things up online from reputable sources. Chat to friends about it. But, as always, check with the professionals before jumping to conclusions.

KEY TAKEAWAYS

- During puberty, you'll get your first period, signaling your body's ability to conceive.
- Each month, your body prepares for a potential pregnancy by releasing an egg and building up the uterine lining. If the egg isn't fertilized, it and the lining are shed during your period.

- Period cramps occur as your body pushes out the lining and can be managed through movement, hot water bottles, or pain relievers like paracetamol.
- If period pain is severe, consult a doctor.
- Hormones regulate your period, and imbalances can lead to PMS symptoms like mood swings or headaches. Severe PMS may indicate PMDD, which requires medical attention.
- Tracking your menstrual cycle with an app can help you anticipate your period and any related symptoms. Expect irregularity at first.
- Choose period products that work best for you. If using tampons, change them regularly to avoid toxic shock syndrome.
- Maintain hygiene by washing externally with water but avoid internal washing, as the vagina self-cleans.
- If you experience dryness or itching during your period, consider using a vaginal moisturizer like coconut oil, ensuring it's safe for use in that area.

Your health and comfort during your period are essential, so don't hesitate to seek support or information!

✳ A Healthy Body, a Healthy Mind

Your body is a lot of fun. It is. Truly.

You can go dancing. Walking. Skiing. Biking with the wind blowing through your hair as you breathe in the scent of summer. If you aren't in a wheelchair. In which case you can do all the above, only slightly differently, but you can move about—get places. Explore things.

What's more, you can eat. Taste. Smell. See. Hear. Discover.

Even if you can't do one of those things, you can do some of them. And you can laugh. And that belly laughter releases chemicals that make you feel like a million dollars.

You can get tickled, receive massages, be caressed, and at some point, experience sex and orgasms.

Your body is a fountain of wonder.

It can also cause trouble. I grew up with asthma and had an immune system that seemed to give in to all sorts of things when I was little. I spent a lot of time at hospitals. And I was still lucky compared to others.

That's why we need to care for our bodies. They need us to look after them to function properly. The mood boosters I so often refer to will help both your body and your mind. Because they work in sync. And how you look at your body will change how you feel about it. Which will change how you feel about yourself. Which will change how you feel about life.

Take a moment. Think about everything your body does for you. Go on. Close your eyes, take a breath, and consider what you can do thanks to your body—from tasting chocolate to reading books and dancing.

You discover the world through your body. You interact with everyone and everything thanks to your body. It's an amazing thing.

Unfortunately, many girls feel they have to look a certain way to be accepted or find a partner. You don't.

What you do have to do is feel good about your body. When you appreciate your body, dress to impress, and show up feeling good, people are drawn to you. You don't have to look perfect, you just have to feel good.

Take a real look around among the people where you live, as well as online. Who is someone with your body type that you find incredibly sexy? Someone who has confidence and poise.

The thing is, people who feel good about their body tend to find others who feel good about their body. If nothing else, simply because they reject the people who don't!

I have the body of a ballerina or model. I'm skinny. I have a flat chest. You can count my ribs. I'm healthy, I'm happy, and I love my body. But I've sat through countless comments about how "real women have curves." They weren't necessarily directed at me, but some people have this idea that women should be curvy. Others have the idea that they should look like traditional models.

> The truth is we all look different, and we should take pride and accentuate what we have, not long for what we don't have.

Make the most of what you've got and enjoy it. Because otherwise, there will come a day when you regret it.

A plastic surgeon, Maxwell Maltz, wrote a very famous book called *Psycho-Cybernetics*. In it he explains the incredible psychological phenomena related to plastic surgery. He said that in cases where the people believed that changing a feature in their face changed their life, it did. In the cases where they didn't, nothing changed. And in cases where people changed their minds without surgery, it had the same effect as surgery.

In other words, Maltz came to the conclusion that it wasn't the surgery that changed people's lives, but their thoughts. Which led to him recommending "shadow boxing" or what I call foreburning to "rehearse" how you want to feel and act in different situations, as well as building confidence through other techniques (such as going through everything you can do well, and every "win" you ever had).

Meaning it's all in your mind.

You can choose to walk around berating your body and seek confirmation from others that your body isn't as nice as it could be. Or you can choose to walk around enjoying your amazing body and find the people who agree with you and feel fantastic. It might take a bit of practice if you aren't used to thinking of your body as sexy and beautiful, but it's possible. And life becomes a lot more fun when you see yourself in this light.

Here's a nice exercise for you to try:

1. Sit down and contemplate everything you can do thanks to your body and your five senses.
2. Find role models with bodies that are similar to yours. If they can look beautiful, sassy, and sexy, so can you.
3. Choose clothes that make you feel beautiful. If you struggle, get people who are good with aesthetics/art to help you out. It needs to feel right but also show you off to an advantage. A nice haircut can also help! A fun thing to do is to find thrift shops and try out clothes there.
4. Sit down every night and imagine yourself feeling beautiful as you play out the next day in your mind.

Note that if you get PMS, you might think you look terrible for a couple of days no matter what because your hormones are acting out. That's when it's time to go for a run or meditate and know that all those horrible emotions will be over in a little while.

Also, apparently, women look their best around ovulation and their worst when they have their period (there's been scientific studies around this), so if you feel down in your dumps when you have your period, don't fret. Again, it will pass in a few days!

There's another level to feeling good about your body and that's eating well, drinking lots of water (or herbal teas), and exercising.

You need about 20–30 minutes of cardio a day, or three hours per week if you do hourly sessions. Use an app for exercising at home, use exercise videos on YouTube, dance around the house, or run or speed walk around the block if you need a quick workout session. Take classes in yoga, dancing, pilates, martial arts, etc. or start doing a sport. Bike to school or walk to school. Join a gym. Start going for hikes. Do whatever you like to get yourself moving.

You should also include strength exercises (push-ups, sit-ups, leg exercises, etc.) a few times a week.

Remember that your body needs rest to recover and build muscles, so if you train your arms today, don't train them again tomorrow. It will work against you. You also need adequate sleep and nutrition to be able to build muscle. Without protein, nothing will happen, but if you don't eat enough carbs, you don't have enough energy to exercise, and if you don't get enough fruits and veg (particularly the latter), you don't get all the nutrients needed for your body to function optimally and heal from the inflammation caused when you work out.

Make exercise work for you. There are so many more options than having to attend one-hour classes or joining a gym. I love exercise, and if I had the time and money, I'd dance every day, but I lead a busy life, and as a currently single mom with work and school commitments, I don't have a lot of time. But I can either charge up the mountain (outside my door) for twenty minutes or play soccer with my kid for twenty minutes every day unless it's pelting down with rain. Then I can jump around the living room or clean like a pro (though that's perhaps not as fun in my opinion) on days when it's raining.

As for what you eat, there's one easy rule to follow: eat whole foods.

What do I mean by that?

Anything that contains preservatives or additives like colorants is not whole foods.

Hydrogenated oils are not whole foods.

Sugar is not a whole food (it's a refined food).

White rice and flour are not whole foods (brown rice and flour are).

Fiber   Fats

Carbs   Proteins

Sausages are not whole foods (chicken and beef are).

That doesn't mean you can't eat some refined foods—of course you can. But stick to whole foods using the 80/20 rule.

There are many different diets out there, but no matter what diet you choose (if any at all), the good ones are made up of whole foods.

Another thing that's important is to get lots of vegetables of all kinds in your diet. You want the full rainbow. Because different veggies contain different nutrients. And both fruits and veggies contain these nifty little things called antioxidants. They fight off free radicals and protect your cells from damage. They're super important.

Nuts and seeds (in limited amounts) are also good for you.

So are legumes (beans, lentils, peas, haricots vert, etc.).

And you need some grains, of the wholemeal variety.

Plain meat is also good (not processed meat like smoked ham, sausages, etc.). How much meat you need is debatable, but if you don't eat meat, you have to be sure to get your protein and essential amino acids from other places, as well as iron and B vitamins.

Eggs also come with some good nutrients and are a good source of protein.

Fish, especially the fatty variety, is good too as it contains omega-3 fatty acids. You don't want to eat fish every day though as it often contains mercury (a toxin), but once a week is a good idea.

The verdict is still out there for whether or not dairy is good for you, but hard cheese and cream don't contain the same amount of lactose found in milk. And yogurt is fermented, and fermented foods contain good bacteria (other fermented foods include kombucha, sauerkraut, kimchi, miso, sourdough bread, and certain cheeses).

While the verdict is also out there for multivitamins and the exact amounts you should take, taking a multivitamin a few times a week is probably a good idea (no more unless you think you need a boost as there is no proof you should take them every day, rather the contrary). So are probiotics and omega-3 supplements (again you might not need them every day). Those are "the big three" where supplements are concerned, but always consult a medical professional before taking supplements.

To sum it up, remember that you need vegetables and fruit for their nutrients, fiber, and antioxidants. You also need an ample supply of protein, carbs, and fats. Olive oil is hailed as one of the best oils for cooking so long as you aren't cooking at too high heat, but you also get fats from nuts and seeds, meat, fish, dairy products, and avocados, among other things.

> When you eat well, you feel well. As a result, it's a lot easier to love your body and feel good about yourself at large.

If you eat the wrong foods, it leads to inflammation in your body, especially as you get older, which can lead to heart disease, cancer, and diabetes. It can also lead to depression and a sluggish brain. As a result, both to prevent disease and issues with mental health, it's important to eat well.

Eating well should also be fun. Find ways of eating well that tastes good! At first, eating less processed foods can feel boring, but once you get used to it, the "fake stuff" starts to taste really, really weird. Besides, with the amount of herbs and spices out there, no meal should ever have to be bland!

A lot of people refer to the Mediterranean diet as one of the healthiest diets, and there's certainly no lack of flavor there!

There are also a surprising amount of treats that are healthy, if still high in sugar, including:

- Bananas dipped in dark chocolate (and rolled in nuts, if you want)
- Freezing smoothies as popsicles
- A ripe avocado blended with honey, cacao, and a tiny bit of vegan milk (or real cream)
- Making chocolate balls made with oats, coconut oil, cacao, a dash of brewed coffee, and honey (you need to melt the coconut oil just a tiny bit)

And even if you like to eat healthy, don't cut all your favorites. On a Friday, have a pizza or burger day. On a Sunday, start the day with pancakes. Just remember the 80/20 rule! If you eat five meals a day, that means four are healthy and one is whatever you like.

KEY TAKEAWAYS

- Your body is incredible, enabling you to explore, move, and create. Focus on appreciating the body you have rather than what you lack.
- **Exercises to Enhance Body Appreciation:**
  - Reflect on all the joys and capabilities your body and senses bring you.
  - Seek out role models with similar body types to inspire confidence in your own beauty.
  - Wear clothes that make you feel beautiful; consider seeking help from those skilled in aesthetics, and explore thrift shops for unique finds.
  - Every night, visualize yourself feeling beautiful and imagine how you want to feel the following day.
  - Cultivate a mindset of beauty and self-appreciation to enhance your enjoyment of life.
- Remember, how you perceive yourself influences how others see you; confidence attracts positivity.
- Treat your body well by incorporating 20–30 minutes of exercise daily, whether through dancing or gym workouts. Both cardio and strength training are beneficial for health.
- Eat a balanced diet rich in whole foods, including carbs, fats, proteins, vegetables, and fruits, to support optimal body function and mental health. Poor nutrition can lead to feelings of sluggishness and depression.

Embrace and care for your body, and your life will become more vibrant and enjoyable!

PART 2:
Building Healthy Relationships

6 BUILDING AND MAINTAINING RELATIONSHIPS

The teens are a period when we often experience conflict. Suddenly we argue with our parents, friends we thought we'd have forever lose interest in us (or we in them), and we often feel pressured to become someone we're not just so we "fit in." So how do you actually build great relationships and stay true to yourself?

That's what we're going to find out!

✳ Emotional Needs

You have emotional needs.

We all do. We all want to feel safe (though we might seek unsafe situations if we felt unsafe growing up). We all want to feel loved (though we might reject it if we feel we don't deserve it).

Gary Chapman, in his famous book *The 5 Love Languages*, explained that through his work, he learned that people needed to be loved in different ways. According to him, there are five main love languages:

- Physical Touch
- Acts of Service (like vacuuming, helping with buying groceries, etc.)
- Gifts
- Words of Affirmation (being told you are loved, being complimented, etc.)
- Quality Time (spending time with a person one-on-one doing things where you really acknowledge each other's presence ... so not necessarily just sitting next to each other watching a movie)

I found this book exceptional when I read it because I understood why I'd felt unfulfilled in some personal relationships with family members and with my ex.

People can buy me diamonds without me raising an eyebrow, but if they spend time with me and are hugging me, I feel loved.

Perhaps, right now, you wish your mom or dad would spend more time with you. Or, perhaps you wish they'd put more thought into the gifts they buy you, or that they'd give you little token gifts throughout the year to make you feel loved. Or maybe you wish they'd hug you more often, praise you, or help with the things you need to get done.

In short, we all need different things to feel loved—people can love us without us feeling loved if we don't get those things. We also have different needs in general to feel happy.

It's important you learn your own love languages, and the love languages of those around you—family, friends, and partners. I believe the quiz for the love languages can be found on his website.

I had the pleasure of working as an editor on the book *Emotional Magnetism* by Sandy Gerber. Working on the book gave me a better appreciation of people's emotional needs In the book, Gerber explains that there are four emotional magnets:

- Safety
- Achievement
- Experience
- Value

People who need safety in their lives tend to buy cars that score high on safety, install smoke alarms, and look after their health. They might also favor very detailed plans, staying in the same city their entire life, and having stable friendships. Trying new things, living on the edge, or doing things without having a plan can be challenging for them.

People who need achievement either go after their goals with gusto, seek acknowledgement through some field, such as becoming an influencer or TV personality, or simply want to be constantly appreciated by those around them even if they aren't very driven. Not getting the acknowledgement they seek can be very unsettling for them.

People who need experience tend to try different jobs or seek a job where there are constantly new things to experience, heedlessly throw themselves into adventure, and come up with date nights that are more elaborate than celebrity weddings … or simply involve an experience. For them, routine can feel like the end of all fun.

People who need value want to know that either they are getting value for their money—buying luxurious things of high quality—or they're getting a deal (i.e. they are getting something for the best price). This also has to do with other things—friendships are seen as investments, so is time spent doing just about anything. Is there a ROI (return on investment)? Will they get something out of it—whether a great friendship, or a pay raise? If not, it's not worth it. If something doesn't add value, they simply see no reason for doing it.

If someone who desires safety goes to a restaurant, they will want to know it's a popular restaurant so that they know the food is good. Or it's a place they often go to, so they know what to expect.

Someone who desires achievement will go to the hottest restaurant in town and hope to meet the paparazzi or some influential people (or the best gaming meetup so they can meet the coolest gamers, or the restaurant they'll get the most praise for picking if going with friends, or a restaurant where the waiters and waitresses know them and will lavish them with praise).

People who desire experience will try out a new restaurant or one that offers a unique experience, such as a place where the waiters are juggling with fire while serving the food.

Someone who desires value will either go to a place that is costly but where the quality of the food is outstanding, or they will go to a place that offers unbeatable prices.

If you, like me, desire experience, the thought of being stuck in one place, having one job, and being in a stagnant relationship will send you screaming out into the streets in a fit of panic.

But let's say I'm dating someone who craves safety. Now we will get along on one level, because I also desire safety. As far as cars, smoke alarms, and healthy foods go. And I like some routines that ground me and stop me from running all over the place. But the thought of planning a trip in minute detail before I travel? It would take away the joy of discovery! The thought of always doing the same things over and over again? Terrifying boredom.

So if I meet someone who desires a lot of safety, I'd have to figure out how to satisfy *his* needs, while also satisfying *my own*. For example, when I went on holiday with my family in my teens or early twenties, they'd opt to stay at the hotel to do sunbathing while I'd head out on some excursion to climb the mountains.

Why is it important to understand our emotional needs?

So we can fulfill them, of course! Otherwise, we'll be miserable, and we might not know why.

It's equally important to ensure one need doesn't become too big. If your desire for safety leads to you locking yourself up at home, something's not right.

Likewise, if your desire for adventure has you dancing with cobras in the desert, perhaps this need for new experiences has gone too far.

Different events in our lives can trigger emotional needs. If you live through a traumatic event, your need for safety might skyrocket. Likewise, if you're bullied, the need for achievement might rise to unprecedented heights. This is when you need to look at taking charge of your emotions, as opposed to running with them!

Try to figure out what emotional magnet you have. I believe Gerber's website still lets you take a quiz so you can find out.

We also have other emotional needs. Such as the need to recharge after a long day. It's important you know what you need to stay balanced. So what makes you feel refreshed and rejuvenated? What makes you feel calm and grounded?

After a long day out with people, I need time for myself. If, on the flip side, I've spent time alone working, it's nice to be social.

You need to learn to watch the signs for when you start to feel "emotionally frazzled" by things so that you don't go into overwhelm. If school is getting so intense that you're feeling panicked, what can you do to let go of the pressure and take time to rejuvenate? If a job feels stressful, do you need a break? What is triggering you to feel the way you do?

We all have different emotional challenges and emotional needs. Some people think nothing of doing ten tests in a week; others think nothing of attending ten parties in a week. But for some of us, one or both could be stressful. So before you reach the point of overwhelm when your emotions get out of hand, step back. Acknowledge how you feel. Breathe. Take time to do something that refreshes you.

KEY TAKEAWAYS

- People express and feel love differently; it can come from physical touch, compliments, acts of service, or quality time.
- It's crucial to meet emotional needs for happiness, but these needs should be balanced. Overemphasis on any one need might allude to an underlying issue.
- Open communication about personal needs in relationships helps prevent feelings of unfulfillment and conflict.
- You can find solutions that meet different emotional desires, such as selecting a restaurant that satisfies both the desire for experience and value.

✳ Understand How to Deal with Conflict

We went through some of this in chapters 1 and 2, when we discussed emotions, and in chapter 4 when talking about effective communication.

First, remember that most people don't act out because they want to be mean. They act out because of something that's happening inside their mind.

If someone is tired, stressed, hungry, or has PMS (premenstrual syndrome, remember?), even small things can trigger them.

Think about a day when you had too little sleep or were really hungry (or both) and then something small happened, making you feel terrible. Maybe you yelled at someone or broke down in tears.

Maybe your baby brother broke your pen, after being annoying all day. And that pen was the straw that broke the camel's back even if you didn't actually *really* care about the pen.

What you needed was calm and perhaps some loving care. What you received was a broken pen.

But your brother didn't necessarily know that you needed some TLC. Even if he knew, he might not truly *understand* it if he's little.

I've been sick with a fever and had a child scream and get really aggressive because I wouldn't do something for him. But I was sick. He should understand I needed care. That I didn't have the energy to do what he wanted. But he didn't. So we both ended up frustrated.

At the time, I felt he was being mean, but he just had a need that wasn't being met, and he wasn't old enough to regulate his emotions or put himself in my shoes. So he acted out to try to get his needs met.

Usually, people get upset because a need isn't met or several needs aren't met.

Those needs can be crucial needs like rest, sleep, exercise, or even food (sometimes when you're hungry, you become emotional).

It can be the big emotional needs like safety, value, experience, and achievement.

It can be the need to feel loved (and if you don't speak their love language, they might not feel your love).

For example, when my little one got upset, it's likely because he's an energetic child (he has ADHD), and having been at home for a day with a sick mummy wasn't fun when he needed to run around to feel good. He couldn't express that, so he just got angry.

Other times, we feel someone hasn't been spending enough time with us, and we start to feel neglected. Without realizing it, this triggers our behavior when we snap at the person for something else entirely.

If they'd just forgotten to call us that day, we wouldn't have thought twice about it. But there were other events that led up to that, which made us think they are neglecting us and don't care about us anymore. And that's why we lash out.

This is why it's so important to take a moment to do one of the mood boosters to avoid saying something we later regret.

In this situation, we need reassurance; we want to know that the person still cares about us and will spend time with us.

Sometimes we have unreasonable emotional needs (it might be our insecurities running the day). But oftentimes, they are the basic needs, and we simply need to express them.

Likewise, we need to learn to understand other people's needs.

For example, if your brother is being annoying all day, why is that? Is he frustrated? Does he need to go out and play to run off some energy? Does he want your attention to see that you care about him? Is he hungry? Is he overstimulated? What does he need?

If you figure out what your brother needs, chances are he will stop being annoying.

Once you see conflict as unmet needs, you can often resolve it easier. That's why communication is so important. Not everyone knows their own needs, but checking in with them and asking questions can help in figuring things out before they become a problem.

Something that plays into meeting emotional needs is the ability to read emotional and social cues. If you can read a person, you often understand their emotional state and can work out what they need. But if you can't read emotional cues, figuring out what people need is really hard.

Let's say you're upset and someone starts laughing at you. That doesn't feel great, does it? But if someone can't read your emotions, they simply think you're pulling a funny face.

Neuroatypical children and adults often struggle with this—they can't read social and emotional cues very well. On the flip side, some people were raised in families where emotions were ignored and don't know how to treat someone who is upset. That might make them uncomfortable, which can lead to things like them laughing or withdrawing instead of the sympathy you crave. And people who aren't great with emotions in general are sometimes more prone to show their care through problem solving, than hugging. This ties into them not having the right social skills.

Social *cues* and social *skills* are slightly different.

Social and emotional cues means picking up on what's going on around you. Like someone being sad, or signalling that they want time alone by withdrawing.

Social skills, on the other hand, is knowing what to do in different circumstances. Someone struggling with social skills might be shy, afraid of what others will think of them if they do the wrong thing, or they just don't know what to do. If their parents were asocial, distant, or had some other issue, they might have grown up without learning how to act around others.

In short, someone lacking social skills or the ability to read social cues acts awkwardly as they aren't sure how to respond to people.

People can still be super amazing even if they aren't attuned to emotions or have great social skills. It just takes longer to get to know them and understand them. If you're struggling with reading emotional cues or don't feel you have good enough social skills, consider reading books, watching videos on the topic, or attending courses.

People often get upset and act out not because they don't care about you, but because they either don't understand how to communicate what they want, they don't understand you, or they think that *you* don't care about them.

This is also why it's important not to explode on someone without first figuring out why they are doing what they're doing.

If they've made you upset, take a moment before you address it. Then calmly explain to the person who upset you why you felt hurt by their actions.

The best way is to do this without accusing the other person. When you launch into how angry you are with them, they'll back away, shut down, or get defensive.

Instead, say something like, "I understand you might not have meant it that way, but when you did X, I felt upset and hurt because of Y. Can we talk about it so that we can understand each other better? I care about you, and I don't want either of us to be upset."

Find out why the other person is upset if they are the one that's triggered. "I understand you're really angry with me. I didn't mean to hurt you, so can you please talk to me about why you're feeling this way? I'm hurting from your anger."

That's very different from screaming, "Stop shouting at me. I hate you." Which resolves nothing.

Being gentle with someone doesn't mean you don't stand up for yourself and set boundaries—if something upsets you, you have to speak up about it. And if it is continuously disrespected, you need to walk away.

Another thing to remember is that not everyone can regulate their emotions. Remember my little boy who started shouting when I didn't do something for him when I was sick? He couldn't regulate how he was feeling because he hadn't learnt to do that yet.

Perhaps you know people who struggle to control their emotions. Their emotions go from zero to 100 in two seconds flat and then they struggle to get into a good emotional state again. They can't regulate themselves. That's, once again, why it's important to learn the different mood boosters. It's also important to remember that when people don't act as you want them to, it's often not personal.

Another tip is to figure out what triggers you. What easily upsets you? Reimagine them in your mind. How would you like to react instead? Practice that in your mind.

Sometimes you can also change your habits to avoid triggers. I get easily upset after seven o'clock at night because I get tired. The better I prepare to have everything ready by seven, the less chance that I get angry if something unexpected happens.

If you get upset *a lot* or struggle to control your emotions, consider talking to someone about it. Perhaps a therapist or cognitive behavioral psychologist can help you take charge of your emotions.

Also remember that if someone close to you gets very aggressive or violent, you need to ensure you're safe. Talk to an adult about it and ask for assistance. There are also hotlines available.

You don't have to stay in someone's company if you don't enjoy it. If someone is consistently mean, rude, or disrespectful, that's not a relationship you want to be in. Sometimes, we have to cut the ties.

Lastly, remember to say sorry when you've done something wrong.

There are many ways to apologize, but if you want to cover all bases:

- Tell someone you're sorry and why
- Explain how you take responsibility for what happened
- Outline how you will use this learning experience to change, or the steps you will take to change
- Make it up to them using their love language, such as buying a gift, offering to spend quality time with them, etc.

KEY TAKEAWAYS

- Often, when someone gets upset, you may be the final trigger rather than the sole cause; their feelings can stem from deeper issues.
- People might struggle to communicate their emotional or physical needs, seeking love and attention without knowing how to express it.
- Insecurities can drive individuals to seek constant reassurance, and it's their responsibility to address those feelings.
- Some people may unintentionally offend others due to difficulties in reading emotional cues or lacking social skills.
- When faced with someone's upset, approach the situation with curiosity rather than defensiveness or aggression.
- If you feel upset, reflect on what you want from the other person, then calmly communicate your feelings and desires, acknowledging that misunderstandings can happen.
- If you make a mistake, offer a sincere apology by explaining your actions, taking responsibility, and outlining how you will learn and change. Consider making amends using their love language, whether through gifts, quality time, or other gestures.

7 MAINTAINING INDIVIDUALITY IN RELATIONSHIPS

Relationships that we have with friends, family, and loved ones can make us feel on top of the world. They can also make us feel really bad, or make us lose track of who we are. So it's important to learn to stay true to who we are and walk away if a relationship is hurting more than it's helping.

✳ Stay True to You

Have you ever felt like you somehow lose your personality when you're with some people? It's like some people bring out the best in us, while others make us feel like we ... disappear.

Some people are really dominant. The alphas or A-type personalities of this world. It's as if they light up a room (or darken it) or just naturally take charge of things.

There are people like that who are super nice, and there are people like that who are not so nice.

The thing is, if you're not as assertive and dominant as they are, you might suddenly find yourself "tagging along."

You're not really into art, but before you know it, you're doing art classes with some fabulous French teacher instead of designing clothes, which is what you really love. Perhaps you tell yourself that you should learn art if you want to become a fashion designer, but should you? Or are you just coming along because, well, you want to be around your friend? Or feel you can't say no to your friend?

Or perhaps you used to do riding. But this friend of yours doesn't ride. She looks at you a bit funny every time you talk about it. And after a while, you stop talking about it. As you spend more time with her, you ride less.

She wants to go out with other friends to do stuff, and you feel you have to tag along or lose her as a friend. Not that she says that out loud, it just *feels* that way.

Sometimes it's not so obvious. You're a kind person. But when you hang out with, let's say, Angela, you find that she often gives little remarks to people. Not exactly mean ones, but they aren't kind, either. Apart from that, you like her (or at least like hanging out with her as fun things happen when she comes along), so you don't stop her from saying those things, even if you don't feel right about them. Perhaps you even find yourself laughing when she says them. Because they're kind of funny, even if they're not funny for the person they were meant for.

Or Angela is the polar opposite of that. She's warm. Friendly. Outgoing. Being around her makes you feel happy. She says nice things about you. She lifts your spirits. And before you know it, you give up on the things you used to love, just to be around her. Just to feel good. And have other people notice you, because they notice Angela.

There are different reasons why we follow these kinds of people and, sometimes without realizing, give up little pieces of ourselves.

Sometimes, it's because they're popular and we want to be part of that crowd. We want to fit in. Have friends.

Other times, it's because we're scared of what they will do if we don't follow their direction. Perhaps we fear losing their friendship or losing the friendship or respect of other people. Worse, we might fear that they will humiliate us, or bully us, if we don't follow along.

Yet, other times, it's because we aren't confident enough to take the lead, so it's nice to have someone else do it. They have the guts to do what we fear. Or we seek reassurance from someone who tells us we're great. We're a bit insecure, and they fill us with so much good energy that it feels like we're walking on sunshine when we're around them.

> The thing is, if you go back to looking into who you are, who you *truly* are, and stand up for that, people will be drawn to you.

This is the reason I say you need a diary. And you need to fill it with things you love. And no matter who you become friends with or who you end up dating, that diary stays. You will not give up on your hobbies, exercising, time with friends and family, or time by yourself, no matter what.

By having a life of your own, you're much less likely to be swept away by someone else. This is because (a) by spending time alone, you remember who you are and (b) by spending time with people who aren't dominating or taking up all available space in the room, you get attention for who you are. You are seen.

This also helps when falling in love. This is because if you're busy, you take time to get to know someone instead of running headfirst into something … and waking up three months later wondering what you've done. When the butterflies start to calm down (that's your hormones going crazy), you realize that perhaps the person isn't so fabulous after all. You were just swept away.

The important part? Create a balanced life. Have things that you do away from certain friends and the person you're dating (if you're dating). Be sure to prioritize people you've known for a long time and whom you love, even when new and fun people enter the picture.

When you lead a life you enjoy, it also becomes easier to say no when someone is doing something you don't want to be a part of. You have a life without them. You also know who you are without them.

The moment you notice you're no longer working on your goals, you're no longer spending time with your close tribe, you're no longer partaking in your favorite hobbies, or you're no longer exercising, or looking after yourself, you know you've lost track.

What also helps is remembering the good things about yourself. What are they? List them and go through them every single day! You're awesome. And even if you haven't figured out all the things that make you awesome yet, you will. So long as you keep reinforcing what you already know to be awesome.

Still struggling to stand up for yourself? The next section deals with more tips for dealing with peer pressure and standing up for yourself in other situations!

KEY TAKEAWAYS

- Some people are enjoyable to be around, leading us to compromise or overlook their negative behaviors.
- Dominant individuals can be difficult to say no to, creating fear of social repercussions if we upset them.
- Outgoing, positive people can overshadow us, making us feel gray or invisible, even though we are not.
- It's crucial to cultivate a life of your own.
- Fill your diary or calendar with personal goals, exercise, mindfulness, hobbies, and supportive friends and family.
- Engage in activities that allow you to shine and express your individuality.

✳ A No Is a No—Rise Up and Conquer Peer Pressure and Bullies

"If I say no to attending Lisa's party, she might not want to hang out with me anymore. But I want to go to a STEM show that day with a girl she doesn't like."

Do you say no to Lisa?

Well, if Lisa can't accept you for who you are, do you really want to be friends with Lisa?

No, you don't. Even if she's funny, has access to all the best parties, and knows that person you have a crush on.

If you say no in a respectful way, showing you'd really like to go, something like, "I'd love to. I really would. But I've made other plans and they can't be changed. So please promise to invite me to the next one?" and she doesn't respect it, then she's not showing you respect. And being around people who don't respect us is a recipe for disaster.

Whenever you stand up for yourself, you risk losing someone. But if you don't stand up for yourself, you risk losing who you are. You also risk losing all the people you'd meet because you are who you are.

When you show up as yourself, others see you as that person. And the people who vibe with who you are will reach out to you.

It's like saying, "If I tell my BF how I feel, I risk losing him. But if I don't tell him, I'll never be fully happy. I also risk losing the chance of meeting someone who would make me happy." Perhaps your BF listens and honors what you're saying. Perhaps he doesn't. Either way, you're better off for having spoken.

It's the same at work. Perhaps it's a decent job, or even a great one, but if people aren't treating you right, is it worth it? Give them a chance. Tell them how you feel in a respectful manner, and see if they change. If they do, great. If not, look for a job that's both great *and* offers a good management team and colleagues. Sometimes you have to wait to express your opinions if you don't have another job lined up, but don't wait forever.

We often fool ourselves into thinking a person or a job is the best thing ever and without them/it, you lose your shot at happiness. You don't. For all you know, the next person or job could be ten times better. You just can't imagine quite how good it will be just yet, because you haven't thought that far!

In our teens, peer pressure can be tough to deal with. Sure, you can stand up to someone, but then what? Have half the school turn against you?

Interestingly, when we do stand up for ourselves, it tends to come with rewards. Other people suddenly see us. We gain confidence. We stop caring about the people who don't care about us. We see the world differently.

Peer pressure can be tough in your teen years, whether it's one person being mean or a group pushing you to go along with something. Here are some tips to help:

- Stay busy with hobbies, family, or other friends so that if things go wrong with the group pressuring you, you'll still have a life outside of it.
- Look for friends or family members who share your values. It's easier to stand up for what you believe in when others believe in you too.
- Talk to someone you trust about how to handle the pressure. They might give you advice or help you feel more confident.

- If you need to discuss a specific topic, read about it or watch videos before having the conversation. Knowing your facts can boost your confidence.
- It's usually easier to express your feelings one-on-one instead of in a group. Confronting someone in front of others might make them defensive, but sometimes you have to speak out when something is serious or dangerous.
- If it's a group issue, find the person who you think will hear you out before addressing everyone.
- If you don't feel ready to speak up, try to avoid situations where you feel pressured to do something you're uncomfortable with.
- When you talk to someone, let them know you don't dislike them, just the specific behavior. People are more likely to listen if you show you're not rejecting them as a person.
- Instead of just pointing out what you don't like, try suggesting what you'd rather they do instead. This can make the conversation more constructive.
- If the pressure involves something dangerous (like drugs or violence) or is hurting your mental health (like bullying), reach out to a trusted adult, counselor, or therapist right away. Even if they don't know the people involved, they can help you find a solution.

Often we don't speak up about something because we're scared we'll end up lonely, or teased, if we do. That's why it's so important to try to find other people in our life to hang out with. People who appreciate us for who we truly are.

Remember the principles we talked about in previous chapters? Stay true to your principles, and how you want to act will become clear to you. Then you just have to find the courage to do so. That can be hard when alone, but remember all the good things about you and do your best to surround yourself with people who believe in you and appreciate you for who you truly are. And if those people aren't in your life right now, they will come.

KEY TAKEAWAYS

- People who respect us allow us to make our own choices and won't be nasty if we choose differently.
- True happiness in relationships comes from being around those who respect our authentic selves.
- Standing up for your beliefs can be challenging, especially in high school.
- Building a life outside of pressure groups reduces dependency on them.
- Talking to someone about the issue can provide support and perspective.
- When confronting someone, prepare what you want to say and do it privately when possible.
- If addressing a group, start with someone who understands your viewpoint.
- Don't hesitate to ask for help when you're unsure how to deal with a situation—guidance from professionals or supportive adults is valuable.
- In dangerous situations, seek help immediately.
- Remember that difficult times can change; you'll meet new people, and things will evolve.

✳ The Knightess, the Damsel, and Your Tribe

Have you ever had an overwhelming desire to help someone? Most of us do.

It's nice to help someone who struggles to walk to cross the street.

It's nice to take a moment and, instead of running home to watch our favorite series, spend twenty minutes or an hour assisting someone struggling in school.

There is a saying, though, that you shouldn't give people fish but teach them *how* to fish.

Let's say you know someone who is irresponsible with money. They ask you to pay for their coffee whenever you meet up because, well, they don't have cash.

Or perhaps you share a room with your sister and she makes a mess but expects you to clean it up.

There are also people who are emotionally not very available or considerate. But we still stick around. We think they're a bit "broken" and we wanna help fix them, because we like them. We might even love them. Never mind that they don't show up for us as much as we show up for them.

> We can't fix people. They have to fix themselves. We can teach them how to fish, but they have to do the fishing.

Assisting someone through a rough patch, being there for people, and helping out is one thing. Consistently being someone's pillar to lean on when they don't offer the same in return is another thing.

The thing with trying to rescue someone is that we don't allow them to step into their power. They need to learn how to rescue themselves.

This is different from having a support network. In a close-knit circle of friends, everyone is helping everyone out. So when Nina has the flu, everyone takes turns to help cook food for her, buy groceries, drive her to the doctor, etc. When she's recovered, she's helping whoever else in the community needs assistance.

This is why it's so crucial to build a great support network, whether with friends, family, or both. Get your tribe together! Foster social connections. It's super important.

We all need help sometimes. We all fall apart sometimes. The important thing is that we don't stay down when we fall down. Because if we do, we're basically telling others they have to take care of us forever.

Some people who want help are also manipulative.

People who try to manipulate us can say things like, "But you always had money. You grew up in a rich family. I didn't. I need you. Please help me out." That's manipulation. They are guilt-tripping you.

Often it's more subtle, "You take care of the cleaning and be a doll. I have so much going on at school at the moment." Sure. If that happens once. But if that's every week ...

"Sorry for cheating. You know how hard I find it to be with just one person. But I love you more than anyone. It's just my mom left me and I ... I don't know. I think I seek attention from different people. Just in case you'd leave me." Well, if they have issues, they need therapy. Or if they want to keep being with different people, they need to be in an open relationship.

Again, if something happens once and a person takes charge from there on, it's fine. We all make mistakes and we all face rough patches. We all need forgiveness and help sometimes. But we all also have to take responsibility as we move forward. And if things happen over and over again without any signs of improvement, then there is no change.

Sometimes it's emotionally distressing. You have a friend who you think might need some therapy—they seem to act out a lot. But you also like them. So you stick around. You just don't want to spend too much time with them because their behavior drags you down. Then they say, "You're my only true friend. Without you, I don't think I could go on." But the responsibility to go on cannot be on your shoulders. It's their life. You can add to it. You can't be *all* of it.

Not all situations are the same.

Some people cannot save themselves. They have mental or physical impairments. They need help. That's why there are often state initiatives or organizations caring for them, or they have a support network of friends and family who can assist with the things they cannot deal with. Perhaps they're great in some areas of life, they just need help in one area. That's fine. That's why we want to create healthy communities where everyone is looked after.

Others can save themselves but don't know how. That's why charities and professionals such as therapists that assist in times of need are essential as they can take care of immediate needs and guide them.

Others also know how to save themselves but don't have the resources as they've faced a challenge. That's why GoFundMe campaigns and similar are so great as you can raise funds in times of need.

The thing is, you can't become responsible for people who are unwilling to learn to do one thing or another. Don't try to be their knightess in shining armor. Especially if helping someone else compromises your well-being.

For example, it's nice to assist a friend with homework and help them do better. If, however, assisting them means you're starting to miss out on all your hobbies, or don't have enough study time to excel at your tests, then it's becoming an issue. They can get help from you, but you can't be the one who ensures their academic success. That has to be them.

This goes two ways. We all have things we'd rather not do. And we all have things we fear we *cannot* do.

That's when we have to break things down. Tackle things little by little. And find the help we need to become self-sufficient.

What can you do if you struggle with something?

1) Ask someone who knows how to do it for advice and assistance.
2) Look up resources for how to become great at it.
3) Break it down. You don't need to walk to the top of the mountain in one day. Turn it into achievable steps.

And remember, when you truly need help—ask for it. We will all run into difficulties at times. These difficulties can be small or big, either way—they're easier to tackle with a bit of help. We just need to learn and grow as best as we can.

Likewise, create a tribe of people whom you are there for. Go out of your way to assist them. Just don't become the crutch someone cannot walk without unless, well, they broke their leg and need your help for a couple of weeks. But remember, that's a few weeks, not a few months, or a lifetime.

KEY TAKEAWAYS

- Everyone falls down sometimes, but a supportive community can help each other rise again; building a support network is crucial.
- Others may depend on you for support, but they must take responsibility for their own lives; you are not responsible for their life.
- Be cautious of manipulative people who may guilt you into helping; don't fall for their tactics.
- Reflect on your own independence—are you overly dependent on someone else? Strive for empowerment by learning to handle your own challenges.
- If you face difficulties, seek professional help, educate yourself, and break tasks into manageable chunks instead of tackling everything at once.

8 ROMANCE—HOW TO DEAL WITH THE BUTTERFLIES

When we fall in love, we think an ordinary person is totally amazing. By the time we fall out of love, we're convinced they are just pure evil. So what's the truth? And how do we deal with all those emotions? And when's the right time to have sex?

❈ Attraction vs. Love

When I was in my teens, and even twenties, I was certain that if I liked someone—if they gave me butterflies—I was in love with them. And the next natural step was a relationship. If someone made me feel good, I wanted to be with them. And I'd make myself miserable pining away for people whom it didn't work out with.

Then I learned about the different kinds of attraction from a friend.

You can be attracted to someone physically (like their body and/or face), sexually (like them in bed), emotionally (you are emotionally compatible), intellectually (you're attracted to their brains, basically), and spiritually (whether you have the same religion or have some sort of soul attraction).

Now, this is not a scientific topic, and I can't say that it's an absolute truth (nor do I know where values fall into this—emotional needs?), but it helps break it down. Someone can be very attractive and smart, for example, but after dating them for a while, you realize that they just don't offer the emotional support you crave.

This made me realize why the butterflies sometimes go away—we're only attracted to one thing or another, not the whole deal (or in this case: the whole human).

You know, you can meet someone and be totally swept away by them. They're just so smart (intellectual attraction), caring (emotional attraction), and good looking (physical attraction). But then you get to know them and the attraction fades away. It's like something's just missing.

Sometimes this is because we're only attracted to someone on a few, not all, of the levels explained above.

Sometimes it's because while a person can be great in all ways personality-wise, they aren't great at relationships (or don't want the same as you from a relationship). Or perhaps they aren't speaking your love language (if that's the only issue, you know how to fix it now that you know what the different love languages are!). (I guess this ties into being emotionally compatible.)

At other times, we want different things out of life. If someone wants to live in rural Mexico building irrigation systems and you want to design fashion in Paris, it's a clash.

There's also everyday life. What does your perfect day look like? What does their perfect day look like? If they want to end each day in a bar and you want to be at home watching Netflix or reading a book, that's a clash. Unless you're okay with spending evenings apart or compromising.

When you meet someone, ask yourself:

- What is it I like about them?
- What is it I don't like about them?
- What do they want out of a relationship?
- What are their goals/dreams in life?
- What does their ideal weekday and weekend look like?
- What's their love language?
- What are their main emotional needs and values—do they like routine, adventure, getting things for value, etc.? Are they big on honesty, playfulness, etc.?
- As the relationship progresses, you have to ask other questions: what kind of home do they wish to create, how do they want to raise kids, how do they want to manage finances, and so on.

You can write down some of this for yourself, too. Then you can compare and see if it matches! Plus, you'll know what you're looking for up front when meeting people!

Remember that we can learn other people's love languages, and just because you like to travel and they don't, it doesn't have to be a deal breaker. Likewise, if they like weekends at home and you like to be out and about, it's not necessarily that you aren't a fit. You just have to see if you can, and if you're willing to, work around it.

Science has shown that when we first meet someone, various feel-good chemicals are released. Those chemicals make us feel so good we easily miss the not-so-good things about a person.

This is why it's incredibly important to keep your own life and not get completely swept away by someone (as mentioned, that diary of yours should be full).

I've also heard it said that using things like the mood boosters mentioned in previous chapters are important to ensure you don't get completely swept away by happy chemicals, only to then "come down to Earth" and feel miserable (even if you like the person!). By doing things that naturally make you feel good, you are less likely to get a "high" from whoever you have a crush on and, later, less likely to feel "down" when the honeymoon period is over.

That said, there invariably comes a dip (even if it's much less of a dip if you do the things mentioned above) when we no longer see the world through rose-colored glasses. Then it's easy to think that the attraction is gone. It's not. You just have to do exciting things together—experience new adventures together and have fun.

Now, we've spoken about some things that can attract you to a person, but how do you know if you love them?

First of all, do you respect them? Are they a person who makes decisions you respect? Do they treat you *and* others nicely? Are their values ones you can get behind?

Secondly, how's your relationship with them? Do you feel they treat you well? Show up for you while still having their own life? Are you creating a life together that you both love?

You can love a person without being in a relationship with them, but you need to love the relationship to be in it.

If you don't truly respect a person—appreciate their values and how they interact with the world and the people around them—chances are you don't love them.

When I refer to love here, I refer to love in the sense of the kind of love you feel for a person whom you want to be in a relationship with. We can love all humans—once you understand that people's biology and experiences make them who they are, it's hard not to love them.

Even if someone has lost their way, you can see that they were once a child seeking love and safety, joy and happiness, just like everyone else. You can love them as you can see the human in them. However, that does not mean you want to be in a relationship with them. It doesn't mean you want to be friends with them, or even be anywhere near them. Because relationships are not unconditional.

For example, you can see the humanity in a violent person who struggles to control their emotions because (a) their brain chemistry is so to speak abnormal and (b) they were raised in circumstances that made them think they have to fight to survive. But you can't be in the same room as them unless it's in a protective environment where there are professionals who can help handle them.

To love someone whom you wish to be in a relationship with, you have to feel a genuine respect for who they are, the values they have, and the actions they take. None of us will agree on everything, but to build a life together with someone, there needs to be a solid foundation of love. You need to love them for who they are, not who you want them to be, not who you think they can be, but for who they truly are right now.

Remember that you can date and have fun with people without wanting to be in a relationship with them. Just make it clear up front what you are looking for. And ask them what they're after. It's not fun to find out after two months of dating that one of you want to date casually and the other one wants a relationship!

KEY TAKEAWAYS

- Attraction can be intellectual, emotional, spiritual, sexual, or physical.
- Sometimes what feels like love is merely attraction to certain aspects of a person, leading to frustration when deeper needs aren't met.
- For a successful relationship, it's essential to build a connection based on common goals and aspirations.
- Initial feelings of infatuation can cloud judgment; maintaining balance through mindfulness, friendships, and exercise can help us see someone clearly.
- Love differs from mere attraction; you can love anyone by recognizing their humanity.
- True love for friends or partners requires mutual respect and compatible values.
- Dating for fun is . . . fun, but if you want to have a relationship with someone, you need to love both them and the relationship you create together.
- Creating a healthy relationship involves fulfilling each other's needs while maintaining individual lives.
- When meeting someone, consider who they are and what they want out of life and relationships, not just the butterflies they give you.

✳ Healthy Dating—the Importance of Slowing Down While Still Having Fun

No one wants to listen to the bores who tell you to slow things down when you're in love—why wait to have fun? Why not spend all the time you have with the person who makes you feel over the moon?

Because once the "high" wears off and those rose-colored glasses fade, you suddenly discover that (a) the person wasn't really who you thought (for better or worse) or (b) you've lost contact with friends, neglected family, have lower grades, your hobbies have been cast aside, and your fitness levels are tanking.

Okay, so it might not be that bad, but it could be. So here's one ground rule I have and one I want you to remember: Never rearrange your schedule for someone until they've proven they're worth it.

They've not proven themselves by sending cute messages or voice notes.

They've not proven themselves by looking good in those jeans.

They've not proven themselves by having the most amazing voice you've ever heard.

They've not proven themselves by giving you a cool gift or taking you on one cool date.

They've not proven themselves by just being fun to be around.

They've proven themselves when they show up (in a good way) consistently. And not just when it's fun, but when it's difficult.

Do you know what they're like when they're stressed?

Do you know what they're like when they're angry?

Are they willing to solve conflict?

Are they willing to go out of their way to help others when needed?

Are they willing to take responsibility for their life and sort things out, even when the going gets tough?

Are they willing to put down the phone and have a proper conversation with you, even if the conversation isn't fun?

You won't discover these things overnight. It takes time to get to know someone. So to say you've fallen in love at first sight … well, you've fallen in love with your impression of a person.

Let's repeat that: You've fallen in love with *your* impression of someone.

Your impression is not who they *are.*

Your impression is who you *think* they are.

There's a difference. And discovering that difference will take time.

Remember those rose-colored glasses? That's your hormones going ga-ga because you feel attracted to the person. It makes you think they can solve all the world's problems with a smile.

That's a wonderful feeling. You should treasure it. But you can do that while going slow.

KEY TAKEAWAYS

To have a healthy relationship, first create a healthy life for yourself.

By staying busy and prioritizing your own life, you stop yourself from rushing headfirst into something you'll later regret. It helps you to get to know the person, instead of falling in love with an impression you have of them.

Once you get to know someone and fall in love for real, you'll experience some really wild butterflies!

✳ Let's Talk About Sex

This section gives you information about sex so that when you decide to have it—be that now or in the future—you have an understanding of what you need to know.

When we hit our teens, or just before, we often start feeling stronger sexual desire. This kind of desire comes about because of our changing hormones. Suddenly a touch from someone can send a shiver of pleasure down our spine and make us feel a desire to get touched more intimately. This is perfectly normal—it's just your body responding to physical stimulation.

However, touching someone in a sexual manner is different and is usually reserved for those you want to get intimate with. You can also feel arousal by looking at someone you're attracted to, seeing a picture of someone who is naked, or seeing someone naked in real life. This is called "visual stimuli" (that means visual stimulation) and is also normal.

You might find yourself daydreaming about sex. In fact, in your teens, chances are you'll start fantasizing about sex, even if you're not in love with someone. Your hormones are simply running wild, announcing you're fertile, and that you should find yourself a partner. It's part of your biology. This can lead to masturbation, which is also perfectly normal.

While it's normal to feel desire, it's important not to act on it without thinking it through. Just because you're attracted to someone and have a desire to have sex, it's not always a good idea to go through with it. Hormones can make us want things that aren't healthy. This is, again, why it's so important to lead a healthy lifestyle as it tends to help us "balance" our hormones.

Remember in previous chapters how I explained that acting when we're really angry or really excited about something might lead to actions we later regret? That's why it's best to take a moment to breathe, or go do something else, before acting on our ideas. It's the same with sexual desire. You need to know that you're safe with someone and that you truly want to be with them before you act on the desire you feel.

If, at any time, you find that your fantasies are becoming too invasive, include themes you're not comfortable with (basically fantasies you don't like having, or feel are inappropriate in some way), or if you don't feel any attraction to men or women, it could be worth seeing a therapist. You might have experienced some trauma, or you might have some form of hormonal imbalance, and asking for help can help you in overcoming it and navigating through it.

Please remember that even if it feels embarrassing approaching a therapist, it's important you do so if you worry about having intrusive (too many) or inappropriate (taboo) sexual thoughts. They're not there to judge. Their job is to help you. And by seeking help, you can avoid both shame and future potential issues.

If you find yourself attracted to the same sex, both sexes, or no one, you should also consider if you want to discuss it with someone experienced in supporting the LGBTQ+ community. Sometimes being in the minority can feel difficult to deal with and having experts guide you can go a long way to making you accept yourself and grow confident in who you are.

Understanding Sex

Sex is often considered to be vaginal penetration. Meaning a man inserts his penis in the vagina of the woman during sex. But it also includes any activity where you get naked with someone and stimulate their genitals, whether with your hands, mouth (oral sex), or your own genitals. Anal sex is also considered sex.

Some people also explore "dry humping" before having "real" sex, meaning they explore each other's bodies without removing their clothes.

The first time a woman has penetrative sex, her hymen stretches and, sometimes, breaks. Your hymen is like a little skin flap, and when it stretches or breaks, it can be painful. It can also cause bleeding. It shouldn't be a lot of blood, and it should stop within a day or so. If you bleed a lot or it doesn't stop, you have to see a doctor right away. Likewise, if the pain doesn't go away after having sex a few times, you should see a gynecologist. Normally, if there's pain, it's because the hymen hasn't broken and needs a little help from a doctor to do so.

Look, the above are more "clinical" or "dry" descriptions of sex and losing your virginity as a woman. In reality, sex is a way for two people to connect and pleasure each other. And even if there is a bit of pain the first time for most women, that pain quickly goes away and sex simply becomes pleasurable. The important thing to remember is to choose to have safe sex with partners you feel completely comfortable with. Then, sex becomes an absolute joy.

Risks and Protection

Having sex comes with risks as there are sexually transmittable diseases (STDs). Some of these diseases spread through bodily fluids and *can usually be prevented by the use of a condom* (granted you don't perform oral sex without protection) while others spread through skin-to-skin contact and cannot be prevented by condoms alone.

The bad news? STDs are really common. The good news? Most STDs won't even give you any bad symptoms so long as you treat them quickly and they can be cured with a bout of antibiotics. This is why regular sexual health checkups are super important.

STDs that are left untreated, on the other hand, can cause very bad health problems, so always get tested!

Unfortunately, not all STDs are curable, which is, again, why testing is so important.

> If you and your partner get tested before having sex, you know you don't have anything to worry about!

Also, remember, you won't necessarily become infected just because you have sex with someone who has an infection or a virus.

Now, let's have a look at different STDs, how they are spread, and how you can prevent them!

STDs that spread through skin-to-skin contact include:

- **HPV (human papillomavirus):** There are many different strands of the virus, some cause cancer, some warts. Most sexually active adults will contract the virus at some point, but the body normally clears it by itself without you even having symptoms. Many women have now been vaccinated against the more harmful strands of the virus. The virus can be transferred when touching someone's genitals. Women should do pap smears every 3–5 years to test for HPV. There is no test for men as such, but anal pap smears can be done.

- **HSV (herpes simplex virus):** HSV-1 causes common cold sores, while HSV-2 causes sores on your genitals. There is no cure. You can get infected by someone even if they do not have the sores at the time you have sex with them, or kiss them, because the virus is active just before an outbreak, too. Chances are, if your parents kissed your cheeks when you were little, you already have HSV-1.

- **Trich (trichomoniasis):** Can be asymptomatic (no symptoms) but can also cause irritation and pain in your urinary tract, or vagina, as well as discharge from the vagina. Usually harmless if treated with antibiotics, but if left untreated, it can cause infertility (meaning you cannot become pregnant).

- **Syphilis:** Can cause a painless sore where you were infected, but it often goes undetected and can later cause an array of different health issues. Can be treated with antibiotics.

- **Molluscum contagiosum:** A form of skin disease that causes bumps on the skin and usually goes away by itself, but you should see a doctor because if it doesn't, it can cause some issues. It can be spread by touching the affected area or touching something that's touched the affected area. It can even spread through water in pools!

STDs that spread through fluids spread through vaginal, anal, and oral sex. They can also be spread through blood (usually needles or blood transfusions) and can, in some cases, be spread through other body fluids.

STDs that spread through bodily fluids include:

- **HIV:** A virus that breaks down your immune system, but today can be managed with medicine so well that someone taking their medicine properly is no longer contagious and the virus can't even be detected (their viral load is suppressed)! If left untreated, on the other hand, it can lead to AIDS (the advanced form of the disease) and death. If you find out you've had sex with someone with HIV, talk to your doctor *immediately* to try to prevent infection as there's now medication for that, but it has to be taken as soon as possible after sex.

- **Hepatitis B:** Most people today are vaccinated, but if you contract the virus, there is no cure. It can cause damage to your liver.
- **Chlamydia and Gonorrhea:** These are the two most common STDs and are bacterial infections transferred through fluids via sex. They can easily be treated with antibiotics but require testing as they often do not present symptoms.

Regular STD testing is vital as most STDs don't create symptoms initially but are easily treated with antibiotics. STDs have been associated with stigma in the past, but it's important to understand that it's no different from catching the common cold. It's just that these diseases are more commonly transferred through sexual interaction, or kissing, and therefore they've been seen as embarrassing.

I'm not telling you about STDs to scare you, but to teach you to practice safe sex. If you do, you shouldn't have to worry about the majority of STDs. And the last thing you want to do while having sex is worrying! You want to relax and enjoy the time with your partner.

Contraceptives

If you do not wish to become pregnant, you MUST use contraceptives. The condom is the easiest method and can also help prevent *some* STDs, but it's not foolproof when it comes to preventing pregnancy as it can slide off or break. That's why some people combine it with a spermicide (a lubricant that kills sperms), but that might irritate your genitals. Emergency contraception (i.e. the "morning-after pill") can also be used if a condom breaks.

Different forms of contraceptives include:

Hormonal Methods

- **Combined Oral Contraceptive Pill (the Pill):** This is the most common type of birth control. It contains estrogen and progestin, which work together to prevent ovulation (release of an egg). It can also thicken mucus in the cervix (the part of your body that connects the vagina to the uterus) to make it harder for sperm to reach the egg.

- **Progestin-Only Pill (Mini Pill):** This pill contains only progestin and works primarily by thickening cervical mucus and may suppress ovulation.
- **Contraceptive Patch:** This releases hormones similar to the combined pill through the skin.
- **Vaginal Ring:** This flexible ring inserted into the vagina releases hormones over time.
- **Depo-Provera (birth control shot):** This injection delivers progestin every 3 months to prevent ovulation and thicken cervical mucus.
- **Implants:** These thin rods inserted under the arm release progestin for several years.
- **Emergency Contraception (EC):** The morning-after pill is most effective when taken within 72 hours of unprotected sex and becomes less effective over time.

Barrier Methods

- **Male Condom:** This sheath covers the penis to block sperm from entering the vagina and can prevent sexually transmitted infections (STIs).
- **Female Condom:** This pouch-like liner fits inside the vagina to block sperm from entering the cervix.
- **Diaphragm:** This shallow, dome-shaped cup is inserted into the vagina to cover the cervix and block sperm. It needs to be used with spermicide.
- **Cervical Cap:** This small, silicone cap fits snugly over the cervix to block sperm. It also needs to be used with spermicide.

Natural Family Planning (NFP)

- **Fertility Awareness-Based Methods (FABMs):** These methods involve tracking your menstrual cycle to avoid sex during your fertile window (the days you can get pregnant). This is NOT a safe method, especially in your teens when your cycle can be irregular.

Intrauterine Devices (IUDs)

- **Copper IUD:** This T-shaped device inserted into the uterus releases copper to prevent fertilization.
- **Hormonal IUD:** This releases progestin to thicken cervical mucus and may also suppress ovulation.

Before you use any of the mentioned methods, you have to look it up to understand the risks and how safe it truly is. For example, most people think of condoms as being safe but they are not 100% effective as they can slip or burst. Hormonal methods, on the other hand, come with side effects, such as a higher risk of blood clots.

Many towns have sexual health clinics where you can get advice as to what contraception to use. You can also book an appointment with a gynecologist to have an exam and talk to them about sex and contraception. It is very important to work with a healthcare professional to ensure you get guidance to make the best choices for your circumstances.

Today there are also so many videos and blogs where women and doctors talk about what you need to know before having sex, so if this feels like too much information, look things up little by little.

Sex should be fun, and to be able to relax and have fun, you need to know you use contraception that works for you. So invest the time you need to figure out what that contraception method should be!

Emotional Considerations

Having sex for the first time is a big event for most women—it's extremely intimate and can feel both wonderful and frightening. That's why it's so important to ask yourself if you are ready for it and if you know how to protect yourself from STDs and prevent pregnancy. You should also feel comfortable talking to your partner about safe sex and ensuring they respect your wishes.

Questions to ask yourself before you have sex:

- Do I know what STDs are and how they are transmitted?
- Am I aware that not all STDs can be prevented with a condom and by avoiding oral sex?
- Am I okay with using (and able to access) emergency contraception if needed?
- How do I feel about abortion and is it legal where I live?

- Am I aware of the effectiveness, as well as potential dangers and side effects of different contraceptives?
- Can I talk to my partner about safe sex and trust them to respect my wishes in the bedroom (not just when it comes to practicing safe sex)?
- Do I have emotional support (someone to talk to) if I become emotional after sex?

There are many more things to learn about sex, such as how to give and receive pleasure. This is not a book about that, but don't be scared to learn. Ask questions. Educate yourself. Have fun!

Sex is nothing to be scared of. It's just something you want to know about before you do it, and be sure to be with partners who practice safe sex and respect you and your wishes.

On that note, remember that no one should EVER pressure you into having sex. You can change your mind about wanting sex at any time, and your partner needs to respect that. Walk away from anyone who tries to manipulate you into having sex with them by threatening to leave you. They are not a person you want in your life.

Please note that I'm neither a medical doctor, nor a sex therapist, so please find out more about sex than what I've written in this chapter from qualified professionals.

KEY TAKEAWAYS

- Sex is the most intimate physical act between partners and can be nerve-wracking the first time.
- Being with someone you know, respect, and who cares about you can make the experience incredible rather than frightening.
- It's essential to be sure you're ready before having sex; answering the chapter's questions can help.
- Understanding STDs is crucial; up to 1 in 4 teens contract them, and some spread through skin-to-skin contact.
- To stay safe, ensure your partner has been tested and consider vaccinations (e.g., Hepatitis B, certain strands of HPV).
- Familiarize yourself with contraception options and their respective pros and cons.

❋ A Short Note on Breakups

In our teens, when we fall in love, it can feel like all or nothing. We want that person. We think they're the one and only. If things end, we think it's the end of all things.

It's not.

You will feel bad for a while.

It will hurt for a while.

Even when you've moved on, you will have moments of hurt when you see the person or when something reminds you of them.

The hurt will slowly go away.

You have to face it (you can't hide from it), but facing it doesn't have to take more than five minutes. Sit with the pain. Then allow yourself to move on.

Do the things that nourish you—that are truly good for you. Exercise. Spend time with friends. Engage in your hobbies. Spend time in nature. Eat good food that makes you smile. Do mindfulness exercises. Watch funny movies. Go to the theater.

No, none of that necessarily feels great at first. You might feel sad when doing something. You might be bored. You might not really want to engage with others. Or even get out of bed.

That's when you have to say, "I'm gonna do it, because eventually, it will make me feel better. Besides, anything is better than lying in bed, thinking the same sorry thoughts over and over again."

Eventually, the time will come when stepping outside and seeing the sun makes you smile again. Or you get a burst of joy from having a bite of your favorite candy. Or you get dizzy with happiness from dancing with friends. And in the meantime, you have to be patient and keep doing the stuff that will bring your happiness back that much quicker. If you don't do those things, it can take much longer, and you might even end up depressed if you get stuck in a negative thought pattern.

As we get older, breakups tend to get easier. It's always hard to lose someone, but if we've survived it once, we know we can do it again. We know the joy will return. We know we will fall in love again.

If you struggle after a breakup, don't be scared to ask for help. Ask your parents to include you in some activities that force you to meet other people (and get out of bed). Ask your friends to spend some time with you so you don't have to be alone. Chat with a therapist about how to move forward.

It's your life. Take back your power. You can and will be happy without your ex!

But what if it's the other way around? You want to break up, but your partner doesn't? Well, if it isn't a fit, it isn't a fit and they have to respect that.

You might be scared of hurting their feelings, but not wanting to date someone isn't about rejecting another person—it's simply saying it isn't a fit for you.

That's the thing with dating: if the shoe doesn't fit, it doesn't. It's not a sign someone is a bad person, can't be loved, or isn't desirable. It just isn't a fit!

And when you date, both parties have to respect that the other person has the right to say no and walk away. If someone can't handle that, they aren't ready to date.

You both have to take responsibility for your own lives, and your own feelings. That's why I keep repeating how important it is to have your own life and fill your diary with things you love doing and things that move you in the right direction in life, so you can get to where you want to be.

You shouldn't "need" another person to feel good and enjoy your life. Another person can *add* to your life, but they can't *be* your life.

Your partner is responsible for their feelings, just like you are responsible for yours.

There are instances when you might meet people who aren't emotionally ready to date … yet are dating. And perhaps you only learn later that they weren't really ready (another reason to take things slow). That's unfortunate, but you can't stay with them because you feel sorry for them. That won't serve them. They need to learn to stand on their own two feet.

If you break up with someone who threatens to harm themselves in any way (worse yet: harm you!), speak with an adult right away. Make sure it's an adult who either informs your ex's parents, or a counselor at school who can inform your ex's parents. If you believe there's cause for concern that the person might injure themselves right away, call the authorities immediately.

No one should emotionally blackmail you to stay with them by threatening to do one thing or another if you break up. And if you find it hard to stand up to them, speak with someone you trust who can help you out. Worst-case scenario, you might have to break up with them in front of a counselor or someone else who can help ensure they get the message.

If you are at any time worried someone will harm you if you break up with them, immediately speak with an adult and the authorities. You have to get help right away. Some people say stupid things they don't mean when they're angry (ever shouted at a sibling that you're going to murder them, for example?) and don't mean a word of it. Usually, you can tell if someone is just blowing off steam or actually mean what they are saying, but please, if anyone ever threatens you, immediately seek assistance from an adult. These are not things that can wait.

Of course, there's breakup etiquette to bear in mind, too. In other words— there are things you should do to break up with someone nicely (and things you shouldn't do!).

First of all, don't ghost people. Be nice enough to tell them you're breaking things off.

Secondly, do it in person whenever possible. Breaking up over text is a coward's way out, and the other person will likely be upset you didn't care enough to do it in person.

Lastly, do it nicely. Explain why you want to break up, but do it without blaming and shaming. Presumably, if there was an issue with the relationship, you've already explained it and tried to fix it with your partner. Either it couldn't be fixed or there's some other reason for breaking up. Often we simply evolve in different directions, or we discover that there isn't actually that much attraction once the butterflies have gone away.

Remember, you can tell someone you like them even if you're no longer in love with them. Just don't give them false hope that things will work out some time in the future, unless you think they will. It's better to make a clean break so that you both can get on with your lives, unless you genuinely think you'll get back together some day.

Oh, and there's something to be said for timing. If someone just lost their dog, wait a day or two (NOT a week or two unless it's extraordinary circumstances!) to break up. I'm not saying you should fake your feelings, but adding a breakup on top of a dog dying the same day is maybe a bit much.

At the end of the day, when it comes to relationships, you have to do what's right for you. Stand firm in what it is you want. And if you feel you can't stand up for yourself, then seek help. See a therapist or counselor about it. This might not be because you're not strong enough to break up, but because something's happened that's making it difficult to come to terms with breaking up. Perhaps you ended up dating your best friend, they just got diagnosed with cancer, and you've discovered you're no longer in love with them but want to keep being their friend.

How do you even begin to navigate a situation like that?

That's when professionals can be of immense help. And, remember, it's not always you who need help. Your partner could be the one needing the help. Perhaps you're dating someone who is going through something really traumatic, like losing a parent, and can't cope. They become depressed or act out in some other way. You still want to date them, but you realize they need help. Then speak with them about it and ask that they do seek help.

Of course, breaking up isn't always a clear cut thing. You could be considering breaking up, but not quite sure if you want to. You're in two minds about it. Then you have to ask yourself if there is anything you and your partner can do to improve the relationship. If there isn't, can you imagine continuing on like this forever?

KEY TAKEAWAYS

- Breakups can be tough as you mourn the loss of someone important in your life, even if they are still around.
- Adjusting can be particularly challenging if your ex was a source of happiness, especially during difficult times.
- It's important to face the pain and gradually engage in activities you love, even if they don't seem fun initially.
- As you focus on positive experiences, you'll begin to feel better and eventually find love again, often learning from past relationships to create something better.
- If you want to break up and your partner tries to persuade you otherwise, listen to them, but ultimately make your own decision.
- Recognize emotional blackmail when someone claims they will be miserable without you; their feelings are their responsibility.
- If someone threatens violence against themselves or others when you want to break things off, seek help from an adult or authorities immediately; safety is paramount.
- When ending a relationship, be kind and respectful: explain your reasons calmly, do it in person, and reassure them that you still care about them as a friend but no longer wish to be together.

9 DIGITAL LIFE

P art of your life is going to be online unless you decide to live as a digital hermit. So how do you foster great online relationships? And how do you create a balance between your actual life and your online life?

✳ Stop the Scrolling Troll—Balancing Online and Offline Life

There's so much you can do online. Between Google and AI, the knowledge available to you is pretty much ... well, all the world's knowledge! Apart from, perhaps, some interesting tidbits in books that haven't yet been uploaded to the Internet.

Of course, a lot of things haven't yet been discovered, and you need physical experiences to learn, too. It's just that the majority of the knowledge humanity has gathered is available online.

How to find the right knowledge, on the other hand, is a bit of a minefield— AI gets things wrong and not every site you find through Google is reliable. That's why you always have to check your sources and confirm facts through other sources.

Getting lost looking for facts about something can be as mesmerizing as scrolling on social media. You just keep digging and find more and more information. That's when it's time to tell yourself you will only look at three or four good sources and that's that (unless it's something like a school assignment, or important research project, that requires more than three sources, of course!).

Most of the time, we don't get lost looking for information, though. We get lost scrolling on social media.

You open your laptop to do schoolwork, but before you know it ... you've spent an hour on TikTok while simultaneously chatting to friends on Instagram.

So how do you stop the scrolling troll—that little voice inside your mind that just wants to watch one more video, read one more post?

There are different ways of doing it:

- **Have an accountability partner:** Tell someone when you're logging on and have them check if you've logged off by a certain time, or challenge each other to limit your daily screen time.
- **Set a timer:** Use your phone or a loud egg timer to remind you to stop scrolling.
- **Log in just before doing something else:** If you check social media right before class or bedtime, you won't have time to get stuck scrolling.
- **Plan ahead:** Set specific time limits for online use each week and try screen-free days to break the cycle.
- **Decide your online purpose:** Focus on meaningful activities like building a following or learning, and set time limits for less productive browsing.

If you find that you are getting FOMO (fear of missing out), you can try joining different offline activities that force you to be present (it's hard to look on social media while ice skating, or swimming, for example).

Likewise, engaging in real-life activities that you *truly* care about, such as saving homeless dogs, can engage you in the moment because the activities are more important than what's happening on social media.

You can also ask your parents or a sibling to take your phone away for certain hours every day or put it in a super inconvenient place, like high on a shelf above the refrigerator for a while.

Mindfulness exercises are furthermore recommended as they help ground you. When you get likes on your post online, or are the first to find out about something, you can get a dopamine hit. That's like a mini-high. Which is why social media can become addictive. Mindfulness exercises help balance your brain chemistry (so to speak), and the need for that "high" becomes less if you're already feeling really good.

Look, online life can be great. It opens the door to connecting with people worldwide. It's really cool. But you have a *real* body and *real* need for human interaction. The kind where you look someone in the eyes while holding their hand or giving them a hug. And the more satisfactory your offline interaction with people is, the less your need for online life will be.

It can feel like offline life is really boring when you have a lot going on online. Who wants to go on a boring coffee date (as in a date with a friend or acquaintance) when you could be discussing styling tips with an influencer who just started following you?

But that boring coffee date with that real person can turn into something beautiful. Because you will need someone to attend parties with, go shopping with, hit the gym with, hold you when you cry, and bring you chicken soup when you're sick. Besides, without offline connections, you'll always feel frustrated because you truly do have a need for real-life connections.

Keep doing great stuff online. You can even involve your "real-life friends" to join you—meet up with them to do stuff together online—but don't forsake the real world for the online world. Because there will come a day when all you want is a hug from a very real, very warm, and caring person.

KEY TAKEAWAYS

- Social media can easily consume hours of your time, so set boundaries to avoid excessive scrolling.
- Try using your devices only before transitioning to another activity, have someone temporarily take away your phone or tablet, or set a timer to limit usage.
- Establish daily or weekly goals for your online time, especially on social media.
- If your online activities have a purpose (like building a business), allocate specific time for them and track how much time is spent aimlessly scrolling.
- Engage in offline activities that genuinely interest you, such as performing, volunteering, or joining clubs, to enrich your life and reduce reliance on social media.

- Remember that social media can be addictive due to dopamine release from likes and interactions, so practice mindfulness techniques like meditation or breathing exercises to promote happiness naturally.
- Regular exercise can also help boost your mood and decrease the desire for constant social media validation.

✳ Managing Your Online Footprint and Security

Managing your online footprint and security these days is a science. There are apps and tech geniuses to handle the big stuff, but we can all become more savvy when it comes to the small stuff.

So let's look at that.

First of all, if it's online, it's there for the entire universe to see.

But it was a private message.

Or it was a post only visible to certain people.

Sure, but once it's been sent or posted, it can be screenshotted and shared with the entire world.

Sure, but people can always repeat what you say, even if it's face-to-face or over the phone.

Yes, someone can repeat a conversation they had with you. But that's different from actually showing an image of exactly what was said.

Hopefully, the people you send messages to or allow to see your posts are good people. But even good people get upset and do stupid things sometimes. And that's why you always have to ask yourself if you truly want to post something online or not.

This is also why you should always take a deep breath before you post something, because once it's posted, it's out there. Are you feeling upset? Over excited? Or are you calm and collected?

Yes, I know. It's totally boring to wait to feel calm, because when you're excited or angry about something, that's when you want to post! But that's exactly when you'll say things you'll often later regret. You weren't yourself. You were in a heightened emotional state. So you said things you don't really believe in.

If you feel really down and want a hug, it's better to ask for a hug than go on a long rant about how you're feeling. Yes, you should be real. But what's the purpose behind it? To get attention? To get care? To get help? Is this the best way? Do you want everyone to know how you're feeling? Or how you felt, two years from now (as they might still remember what you posted)?

Consider if your post will help others in some way, too. Saying you feel fantastic when you don't isn't real. Saying you feel terrible and will sit and feel terrible doesn't help much either. And people might get a negative impression of you. Saying you are feeling down but are doing x, y, z to feel better might inspire others to join you and help themselves in feeling better.

Also, are the posts you're sharing relevant? Does everyone need to know you just cut your toenails? Or is this maybe a bit too much information (TMI)?

What pictures you post of yourself is another thing to consider. It's nice to see people keeping it real, but keep it balanced. Putting the absolute worst photos of yourself out there is no more necessary than only having airbrushed ones.

If something is posted publicly, you also have to be aware that future school admissions departments or employers could check it out. They want to know who you are before accepting or hiring you. And that's when they discover that you bragged about turning in an essay your big brother wrote or love cracking jokes about your bosses. On social media. Where anyone can see it.

Or they just discover you have an Instagram account filled with garden gnomes, or Taylor Swift.

Look, you have to be who you are, garden gnomes and all. Just remember that friends, family, coworkers, and the world at large can see what you post if it's a public post.

Another thing to consider is where to post what.

If you do public posts on Insta, do you want everyone to know where you live and/or work (including any potential future stalkers) or what your baby sister looks like? Maybe that's better for that list of close friends on Facebook.

On the other hand, if you're really into fashion design (or garden gnomes) and want to build a following in that niche, Insta is a good place to post. But friends and family on Facebook might be more interested in your personal posts and updates, rather than fashion.

There are so many different platforms (with more coming all the time), and they all have different uses. On LinkedIn, almost everything is about work, whereas TikTok has a niche for just about anything.

Here are some general tips around security and your digital footprint:

Once you post something online, it leaves a digital trace, even if you delete it. People can still take screenshots and share them, even in private groups.

Never share personal details like your home or work address, or photos that reveal where you live, especially in public posts.

It's cool to meet people online, but be cautious—people might not always be who they say they are. A video call or checking for verified accounts can help, but always stay alert. Online behavior doesn't always match real-life actions, even if you've been chatting for a long time.

Never give out your credit card details to someone you meet online. Before making a purchase, double-check the store by reading reviews or searching for the business. It's safer to use payment platforms like Google Pay or Apple Pay, but always stay cautious. If someone you don't know asks for money online, it's likely a scam (unless it's for something legit like a GoFundMe campaign).

Review your social media privacy settings to know who can see your posts and for how long. If your posts don't disappear automatically, regularly go through your accounts to remove things you no longer want visible.

Use strong, unique passwords for each site, and turn on two-factor authentication (2FA) to prevent hacking. Avoid easy-to-guess passwords like your name or birthday, and always keep your devices in safe, secure places.

Social media can be fantastic—you can meet people from all over the globe, start a business using your following, or launch a campaign for homeless people, or even raise funds for yourself or a friend when in need. You just have to stay safe and beware of the pitfalls.

KEY TAKEAWAYS

- Be aware that when you post online, others can screenshot and share your content, leaving a digital footprint even if you delete it later.
- Check your privacy settings across different platforms to control who sees your posts, and consider creating lists for selective sharing.
- Different platforms serve different audiences; tailor your content accordingly (e.g., friends and family on Facebook vs. specific interests on Instagram).
- Before posting, assess your emotional state. If you're upset or overly excited, wait until you can think clearly.
- Reflect on the purpose of your post. Ensure it's suitable for social media and avoid oversharing personal details.
- Prioritize safety: don't disclose your home or work address, credit card information, or send funds unless to a legitimate campaign.
- To verify someone's identity online, consider a video call, but remember that online personas may not accurately reflect their real-life behavior or emotions.

✳ Social Media Envy

Ever gone green in your face when looking at someone's social account? They just live in such a gorgeous place and have such incredible adventures. Perhaps they even look perfect.

Chances are this perfect person is not perfect at all. Influencers, for example, often have people who manage their online persona. Yup. They have to say and do certain things to make sure their followers like them. They also avoid showing some of the things they say and do for the same reason.

Even if someone isn't a big influencer, you probably won't see what they look like at 5 a.m. on social media. And with the amount of filters people use today, finding anyone who looks like themselves in real life is a bit of a mission.

Plus, what people show you online is selective. They are much more likely to film the perfect corner of their house than the mess their kids have made in the living room ... where they haven't vacuumed for three weeks because, well, life got busy. But their study is still in perfect order.

Even if someone truly lives a charmed life, they can suffer from insecurities, relationship problems, depression, and a whole array of other issues they do not speak out about.

So when you look at that perfect person doing that perfect dance move, looking utterly amazing, just remember they might have farted and had you been present ... they would not have looked (or smelled) so perfect!

If you start getting social media envy when it comes to some people, first figure out why. What is it they have that you'd like to have? Write a list. Then figure out how to get what you want.

But don't stop there.

Once the list is done, start focusing on what's working in *your* life right now. Write *that* down.

Then go about creating *more* of what you already have and more of what the influencer (or whoever it might be) has that you would like to have.

The more you do the things you love with the people you care about, the less you care about what people are doing online.

Let's repeat that:

> The more you do the things you love with the people you care about, the less you care about what people are doing online.

When you're happy with your life, you see online personalities as a source of inspiration—whenever you see something you like, you start adding that to your own life.

Create a life you love. That's what matters. If things are tough right now, find the golden moments. Even if it's just that you own one book you love. Have one friend who makes you smile. Know your sister cares about you even if she's a pest (in general).

KEY TAKEAWAYS

- Remember that people don't share their entire lives online; even those you admire face their own problems and issues.
- A nice house doesn't guarantee happiness; what someone needs could be adventure, fulfilling work, or meaningful friendships.
- When you feel envious of someone's social profile, shift your focus to the positive aspects of your own life.
- Concentrate on what's working well for you and seek to build upon those areas.

❋ How to Make Friends Online While Staying Safe

I touched upon this a bit in the previous section about your online footprint and online security, but making friends online can be great.

For starters, you can easily find people who are interested in the same things you are. And some places, like TikTok, X, and Insta, are really good for building a niche following.

Facebook, on the other hand, is great for finding groups. Whether you like Spanish cooking or Mexican salsa, there's a group for it.

Moreover, there are support groups on Facebook. My best friend joined a group for moms expecting twins when she was pregnant and that kept her (fairly) sane, as other people faced similar problems and talked about them. They could help each other troubleshoot and feel less alone and overwhelmed (twins are a pretty big deal).

The issue with online friendships?

You don't truly know someone until you meet up in real life.

Look, long distance friendships are nothing new. I grew up with a pen pal in Kenya, and when we finally met in our 30s, we were like sisters. Not every story ends like that, though.

I have used online dating sites, chatted to people, done video calls, and still felt like I met someone different from who I expected to meet.

There are a few things to remember:

- Don't share things with people or in groups unless you're truly okay with that information being made public.
- Only share information if you're okay with it becoming public.
- If you want to verify their identity, get on a video call.
- Even if they look like their pictures, they might not be truthful about their life.
- The impression you get over video may differ from real life.
- You won't know how someone handles stress or anger just from online chats.
- When meeting in real life, choose public places for the first few times and tell someone where you are. Avoid private spaces or risky situations.
- Consider why they're meeting people online—what's their motive?
- Never send pictures you don't want shared publicly.

Of course, if you end up knowing someone for years and do video calls with them and their family, friends, etc. and in different places (when they are out shopping, when they're hanging out with their grandma, etc.), you get a pretty good idea of their personality. Just don't jump to conclusions and *always* play it safe.

Just as you would in real life, take your time getting to know someone online. No one reveals all different sides of their personality in one day. It takes a lot of time to get to know someone well.

KEY TAKEAWAYS

- The internet allows you to connect with many great people who share similar interests or experiences.
- Keep in mind that online personas may differ from real-life personalities.
- A video call is a good first step to truly get to know someone.
- Even if someone seems nice, proceed with caution, as they may not be truthful.
- If you decide to meet someone in person, choose a public place and inform someone you trust about your whereabouts and who you're with.

PART 3:

Academic and Future Success

10 GOAL SETTING AND TIME MANAGEMENT

Dreams are all well and good, but how do you turn them into goals? And how do you break down goals into achievable daily steps? Plus, how do you get it all done without getting overwhelmed? Where do you even start? And how on Earth do you stay motivated? Let's find out!

✳ Goals vs. Dreams ... and That Action Plan

What's the difference between a goal and a dream?

A goal is something you're actively working towards.

Dreams, unfortunately, aren't always very realistic.

I don't mean to say you can't achieve them, what I mean is that they aren't always *based in reality*.

Dreaming about being a world traveler constantly going to new destinations seems ... exciting. But if you've ever spent time traveling, you also know that carrying all your stuff from destination to destination can be tiring. Airports and traveling at untimely hours can also be tiring. Constantly having to say goodbye to people and adjusting to new places can further take its toll. And having your "office" set up in different coffee shops and AirBnBs where the Wi-Fi isn't always working and the sound level is high can get irritating.

That's not to say you shouldn't become a traveler. I'm just pointing out that when we dream about things, we don't always *think them through*.

Once you've thought something through and still dream about it, then you can be more certain that it's something you truly want to achieve.

What is it you want to do in life—what are you dreaming about for your future?

Write it down.

Then think it through. Really put yourself in the position of the person you want to be. Feel what it will be like. If you want to travel to Antarctica, imagine walking in snow boots and in enough layers to feel like the Michelin Man (look it up and you'll see what he looks like if you don't already know). Is it pleasant?

Now, I have no idea what it'd be like to explore Antarctica, but I grew up in Sweden and know enough about the cold to know I'm not a fan of being dressed as the Michelin Man.

I also know that no matter how cute and idyllic descriptions of winter in different places are, I absolutely detest gray skies and short days. I get depressed in an instant, only to reawaken in spring and turn into the Energizer bunny.

Had I not come from the cold dark North, I wouldn't have known those things. And had I not tried living in the hot South, I wouldn't have discovered what difference it makes.

So when you are contemplating your dreams, don't just think about the superficial stuff. Really imagine what it will be like working at the ER for twelve hours straight, chasing a news story at 5 a.m., or not being allowed to party with friends on a Friday night because you're in the Olympic running team.

Some dreams are only fun on a surface level. Being a gold medal Olympic champion sounds great, but can you imagine the work and sacrifice it would take to get there? If you enjoy that work, then it's for you. If you can't imagine doing that much work, then it's not for you.

Dreams can also be dangerous.

There are many accounts from WWI and WWII (and surely countless other wars) where men couldn't wait to sign up and go fight for their country. They saw it as exciting. Heroic. And thought the war would be over in a month or two.

A lot of these men didn't make it back to their homes.

Some came back with what was then known as "shell shock" and is now known as PTSD (post-traumatic stress disorder). They couldn't function in daily life because of the horrors they'd seen and experienced. *Their dream of the war was not based in reality.*

Look, most dreams are not that destructive. But you have to really imagine what something will be like in real life.

And when you dream, see the bigger picture. You might be hyper focused on your career, social life, or love life. But what about the other areas of your life?

It's like dreaming about a wonderful house to live in. That's fantastic. But if all you have is a house, well, life will be empty. What are the dreams you have for love, friendship, career, and hobbies?

Try to approach dreams from a holistic perspective where you don't just focus on one thing in your life, but all the different areas of your life.

Once you've decided you truly want something, you have to commit to achieving it. It's not, "Maybe I'll do it." No, you're *going* to do it. If you're debating whether you can, or should, you're not committed. For you to succeed, you have to commit. Otherwise, you'll give up at the first sign of adversity, and there will always be adversity.

Dreams only turn into goals when we start moving towards them. In the beginning of this book, I spoke a bit about how to break tasks down so that you can achieve them. And that's exactly what you have to do with dreams.

If you want to become a dog trainer, what is it you can do today, this week, this month, and this year, to get there?

Goal: Become a Dog Trainer

Goal This Year: Learn as much as possible and get an apprenticeship/internship with X dog trainer over summer

Monthly Goals:

- Spend at least an hour a week learning from other dog trainers through videos/books
- Read one dog training book per month
- Assist one person per month with training their dog (some dogs might take more than a month to train)
- Put together a resume with my experiences

- ○ Walk dogs to earn pocket money
- ○ Start taking pictures and videos I can later use on social media to market my skills
- ○ Start editing together photos and videos

Goal Next Year: Set up my own blog and start social media accounts

Monthly Goals:

- ○ Spend at least an hour a week learning from other dog trainers through videos/books
- ○ Start Instagram and TikTok accounts in January
- ○ Post one post (for Insta) and three reels/videos per week
- ○ Set up website/blog in March
- ○ Write one blog per month
- ○ Assist one person per month with training their dog (some dogs might take more than a month to train)
- ○ Update my resume
- ○ Walk dogs to earn pocket money
- ○ Study for one hour every day so I know I will get to pick a good college

At the end of each month, you create the more exact monthly and weekly goals for the following month. So that you know what you need to do each week to reach your ultimate goal.

It might seem a bit silly to write everything down in your diary or calendar—you know what to do. But getting into this habit is really, really good. It will help you keep track of things when they get more complicated. Such as when you are running a full-blown dog training business.

I'd also say not to be afraid to use a little bit of intuition when you break down dreams into goals. You think you should go about things one way (logically speaking), but is there a better way? Close your eyes, still your mind, and let inspiration flow. There are some really unusual ways to get to some places in life, and it appears that intuition can sometimes guide us. Or perhaps it's just a bird's eye view—when looking at a problem close up, we tend to turn to the most logical, or common, answer. But when we step back and see the bigger picture, we discover there's a shortcut we didn't see before.

Perhaps that's all there is to intuition—it's putting together everything you know and seeing the totality. Perhaps there's something more to it. I don't know. But I find that stilling my mind, or walking away and coming back to something, helps me see new solutions and ways of doing things.

Now, I know very little about becoming a dog trainer. If I truly wanted to become one, I'd start with asking AI what it's like. Then I'd look up information on Google about the profession. After that, I'd try to find blogs, vlogs, and social media accounts run by dog trainers. I'd also read books.

You might want to start at a different end—go to YouTube and watch videos, then look for blogs, books, and Google articles. Perhaps use AI to ask questions when you come across things that are difficult to understand, like dog training terminology, or asking how to create a business plan for a dog training business. The important part is not where you start, but that you don't just go to one source. A book might be harder to read but give more detailed information. AI might get some things wrong, but it can sum things up in a way that's easy to digest.

It's only after we gather information that we can make informed decisions. And even then, it sometimes takes trying something out in real life to see if it's for us. But remember that meeting just one dog trainer might put us off if we don't happen to like that particular trainer, or his or her particular methods. Just as with sources, try to get a few different points of view.

Here's a good way of checking if a dream is something you'd like to turn into a goal:

- Find out information about it online and through books.
- If you can, try to explore it in real life (like talking to dog trainers if you want to become one and visiting their workplace for a day).
- If you have access to someone who has done what you want to do, ask questions about how they went about doing it, bearing in mind that there are many ways to reach the same destination and another way might be better for you.
- Try to imagine what it will really be like doing what it is you want to do (smells, sights, sounds, textures).
- Consider what you have to do to get there—are those steps you're willing to take?

By the way, remember that TV shows and series aren't real. Yes, they may show real "cases" about what happens inside hospitals, but seeing a doctor perform surgery on TV is different from standing and holding a scalpel in real life ... and with it, holding someone's life in your hands!

That said, shows and series can be great sources of information and sometimes give us real insight into something we wish to do. Be that travel to Mexico or become a mixologist working at Michelin-star restaurants. Just remember that even documentaries undergo heavy editing and you won't get the full picture a lot of the time.

KEY TAKEAWAYS

- Dreams are imaginative and often vague, while goals require action and direction.
- To achieve a dream, it must be transformed into a specific goal.
- Consider the reality of your dream before pursuing it— determine if it's something you'd truly want to do.
- Gather information through books, videos, blogs, and conversations with people who have pursued similar paths.
- Experiment with small actions related to your dream, like shadowing someone in that field.
- Once committed to a goal, take decisive action and be prepared for challenges; adapt as needed but keep moving forward.
- Recognize that life encompasses more than just one dream— explore various areas like friendships, hobbies, and personal growth.
- Set goals across different life areas and break them down into yearly, monthly, and weekly milestones.
- Document your goals, take consistent action, and take time to reflect and listen to your intuition for new insights.

❋ Roadblocks

Every goal, every dream, everything you do comes with roadblocks, mishaps, detours, and an array of juicy problems to solve.

If you wake up and decide to stay in bed all day (on a day where you have no commitments), there are few roadblocks preventing you from achieving it. Until you realize you need food. You're out of ingredients for what you want for dinner. Should you go out and buy ingredients or order food? You try to order food, but the restaurant has an issue with their online payment system and you can't pay them online. You either have to go to the restaurant and pay or go to the shop and buy something else and cook yourself.

Some twists and turns we expect. Others we don't.

One book I am reading about parenting suggested that the one thing we know for certain is that storms *will* come. So the one thing we can prepare for is the storms. (In this instance, your kid having a tantrum.)

Of course, there will also be sunshine. But that, often, doesn't require the same amount of planning as we don't feel down in the dumps and act out because of it. Nor do we have to problem-solve and work hard to find solutions (more about that in the chapter about leadership in the section about innovative thinking).

No path in life is perfectly smooth. There will be obstacles. And a good way to stay positive in life and enjoy yourself is to acknowledge that there will be issues and decide, up front, how you want to feel and act when they happen.

If you think everything will happen as if by magic, on the other hand, you'll be sorely disappointed when it doesn't.

This refers back to what I talked about in the beginning of this book—the stories we tell ourselves when bad things happen.

"I lost my job, now I'll never become Director of that company, all is ruined."

"I lost my job so clearly that wasn't the right position for me. I learned a, b, c from this. Now I'm going to find an even better job, with better pay, and better prospects. I also want a job with more easygoing and fun colleagues."

When the bad news hits you—that slap in your face sensation, the clenching of your gut, and the pain in your heart—it's difficult to feel inspired to think happy thoughts. But that's when you have to (a) do something to raise your spirits (mood boosters) and (b) think about things constructively. What can you do to get to where you want to be in these new circumstances?

My coach always says that when you create things in life, you have to be sure not to pin your outcome on one thing. What he means by that is that if your goal is to build an amazing house, you can't pin that goal on that one plot of land. You can build an amazing house, in an amazing place, even if you don't get the plot of land you currently have your eyes set on. Just like you can create an awesome relationship even if it's not with the person you first thought it would be with. You can have an epic time at college, even if it's not the college you thought you'd end up attending.

Acknowledge the disappointment. Feel it. Then decide that you're going to create something amazing, just differently than how you first imagined. Then get into a good state of mind by doing things that make you happy. From there, start forging a new path towards your dreams.

When a plot twist happens, be aware that negative thoughts will pop up. It's okay. It's normal. Just don't be lured into thinking those thoughts are an accurate view of things, or that you're going to feel that way forever. You won't.

You also have to know that not all dreams come true. And that's a good thing. Because some dreams aren't really for us after all. But if we spend all our time fretting about the fact that life didn't turn out as we imagined it would, we miss what's right here and right now. And those things could open up to even bigger and better things.

Infuse energy into what you're doing right here and now. Especially the things you love. Otherwise, you'll spend your entire life looking at tomorrow.

Moreover, remember to be creative when looking at taking steps to achieve your goals. Thinking outside the box can be really valuable.

For example, your goal could be that you want to improve your social life. Only, you're shy and you feel petrified thinking about doing lots of social activities. You're just not ready to socialize at a big party.

On the other hand, while you're learning about confidence and social skills through books and videos, and attending regular therapy sessions, you don't want to wait till you're a confident social ninja to enjoy some company. You're feeling lonely here and now.

So how do you do something social that's not overwhelming for you?

What do you enjoy? Let's say it's books. So, hang out at the library, join a book circle (even an online one if in person is too much at first, though for some, online groups are actually harder to speak up in), sit and read in a café, or visit local bookshops more often.

Some of those things are more social in that you actually interact with people, others just let you be around people. And if you go to a bookstore, you can challenge yourself to compliment the staff for some of their books or do something else you wouldn't normally do.

In short, try to do things right here and now that bring you joy, even if the "big goal" is still a ways away. And remember in the section about overcoming adversity where I mentioned course correction? Course correction is needed in our pursuit of most goals—you need to ask yourself if you're on the right path and, if you are, find ways of overcoming the roadblocks. More about that in the chapter on leadership, too. Especially the section about innovative thinking!

KEY TAKEAWAYS

- Life is unpredictable, with inevitable ups and downs; accepting this helps manage expectations.
- Recognizing that "downs" are a natural part of life allows for a quicker recovery and a focus on future "ups."
- When faced with setbacks, explore alternative paths toward your goals and seek immediate enjoyment in the present.
- Balance future planning with appreciating the current moment to avoid missing out on today's experiences.
- Reframe the narratives you create about your experiences; strive to tell a positive story about challenges faced.

✳ Time Management

There are things you *have* to get done, and there are things you *want* to get done.

You *have to* do your homework. You'd *like to* work on your dream to become a singer by doing voice exercises and rehearsing some songs to have ready for whenever you might need them for auditions and performances.

So, where do you start?

Time management experts tend to view it this way: put the essential stuff first on your to-do list and schedule a set amount of time in your diary for it. That said, you also have to schedule in the stuff you *want* to do. Otherwise, you'll never reach your goals.

By allocating set amounts of time in your diary for various tasks, you avoid (a) trying to decide what to do next and wasting time and (b) taking too long with something. You also stop sitting around doing nothing, scrolling on social media, or worrying about tomorrow because you have a schedule to follow!

Have you ever noticed how you do things faster when you have a deadline? That's another reason why you should allocate time in your diary for different tasks—it pushes you to work faster.

Here's the next tip: schedule boring stuff just before you need to be somewhere.

You will clean the house much faster knowing that in one hour your date will arrive than you would if you knew you had all day. Plus, if there's nothing fun to look forward to, you might just feel soooo bored while cleaning.

I remember reading this Dale Carnegie book where he talks about a woman who was very bored at work. Then she set herself little challenges—type up this document in ten minutes, get more work done than the other person in the office, etc.—and started enjoying herself.

When you challenge yourself, you feel more motivated and, usually, have much more fun! You also get stuff done a lot faster!

Want even more motivation? Reward yourself by the end of a task. Give yourself ten minutes on social media, a walk with your dog, a call with a friend, or an hour at the gym (whatever feels like a reward to you). If you have many things to do, you can schedule "ten-minute rewards sessions."

Another tip is to consider being of service. When I type this book, I'm constantly thinking about you, the reader, and being of service to you. I want my experience and wisdom to serve you. When I work on materials for businesses, I want my work to serve the business and the people behind the business. When I assist my kids with stuff, I want to be of service to them. When I go for walks, I want to be of service to my body and mind, as exercise helps me maintain a healthy body and mind.

You can also shift your focus to the outcome—while cleaning is boring (which it usually is, in my opinion), I LOVE having a clean house. Plus, when I clean, I listen to fun audiobooks, and I do my best to move my body as much as possible as I hate sitting still and working. I love my job, but the sitting still bit annoys me to no end. Cleaning, believe it or not, is good exercise if you put some effort into it!

So, while I don't particularly like cleaning, I do like getting a break from work for ten minutes and getting some exercise while at it. Plus, I really enjoy listening to audiobooks, and I get to do that while cleaning.

So that's another tip—if you don't enjoy something, try to make it more fun somehow.

Productivity is also about energy. In past chapters, I've spoken about how important it is to eat well, exercise, get enough sleep, spend time in nature, do mindfulness exercises, and so forth. Those things will help you be much more focused.

Feel unfocused right now? Take ten minutes to go for a short but fast-paced walk, then sit down and do breathing exercises for five minutes. Chances are that by the end of the fifteen minutes, your mind will be a lot clearer. Also remember that you need food and drink to keep a clear head! If your blood sugar levels go down, your mind can get fuzzy.

Of course, to focus, also helps to turn off the distractions. Walk away from your phone and TV if you have a task that requires your focus. I find that instrumental music works well, but I can't do lyrics when working.

Also remember that your mind tends to be the clearest in the morning, so for tasks that require brainpower, try to get them done early on in the day. Breaks throughout the day are also essential. In fact, a few ten-minute walks during the day can likely help improve your productivity!

To recharge, you also need time for fun! Schedule it in!

Feeling overwhelmed? Remember what we did with your goals? Break it down. You don't have to climb a mountain in a day, just take a few steps up the hill! Most of us can handle doing something, even something we don't like, for ten minutes. And by tackling it in ten-minute sessions we can get through just about any task.

KEY TAKEAWAYS

- Write down tasks in your diary or calendar, allocating specific time slots for each.
- Prioritize top tasks first; ensure they get done.
- Schedule time for personal goals and enjoyable activities to prevent neglecting them.
- Challenge yourself to improve efficiency and make tasks more engaging.
- Tackle boring tasks just before other commitments (like catching the bus) to speed up completion.
- Use rewards as motivation; complete less enjoyable tasks before enjoyable activities, like seeing friends or checking social media.
- Make tasks enjoyable by incorporating music, audiobooks, or something else that you enjoy.
- A lot of people are the most productive in the morning, so aim to get important tasks done then (or whenever you're the most productive). Also, be sure to take breaks and stay hydrated and nourished throughout the day.
- Prioritize fun, relaxation, and adequate sleep for overall productivity.
- If feeling unfocused, ensure proper nutrition and take a 10-minute brisk walk followed by breathing exercises.

11 CAREER AND FUTURE PLANNING

How do you decide what career to pursue? And how do you prep for college and/or leaving home? Those are questions we'll look at in this chapter!

✳ Career Planning

Perhaps you think a lot about your future career—daydreaming about what it will be like to one day do something.

Or perhaps career is something far off in the future for you—something you'll tackle after college.

Either way, there are things you can do *right now* if you want to find out more about potential career paths and if they're truly suitable for you.

Let's begin with looking at how you can come up with ideas for different career paths that might suit you, in case you haven't yet figured out what you want to do with your life.

Before we start, remember that careers aren't always forever.

First of all, they change and evolve—sometimes going off in unexpected directions. You start off as a secretary at a newspaper and end up as a journalist, for example.

Secondly, if something turns out not to be for you, you can train to do something else. There's always an opportunity to change paths if needed or wanted.

Now, let's look at how to get ideas for a career that'll suit you.

There are a number of questions to answer to figure that out:

- What are my interests and hobbies—the things I love doing?
- What are the things I'm good at skillswise—such as math, carpentry, drawing, cooking, sewing, coding, graphic design, dancing, writing, basketball, etc.?
- What are my soft skills—such as organizing, dealing with people, leading projects, being creative, being analytical, inspiring others, etc.?
- What's my personality like? Am I outgoing, calm, talkative, quiet, funny, motivated, ambitious, etc.?
- What kind of environments do I like? Do I like fast-paced environments that challenge me, or do I prefer a calm pace where I don't feel any pressure? Do I thrive when in a quiet place and left to do my own thing? Do I like interacting with people?
- What are things I would like to avoid—such as having to deal with numbers, organizing things, loud environments, etc.

Answer all these questions (you can list your answers in bullet points). Then try to find a profession where your personality, skills, and interests all come together.

But what if you can't think of a profession that'd suit you? What to do then?

You can ask friends and family to have a look at your answers and see if they have any ideas.

You can ask AI and see if it has any ideas—just plug in the questions and your answers.

While neither friends and family, nor AI, will necessarily come up with the right answer, they can help you brainstorm.

Once you know in what direction you're heading, you have to ask if the career path you have in mind is one you'd *truly* like? Sure, it seems that working as a financial analyst at an investment firm is what would get your juices going as it would involve you using all your strengths. But will it truly work out?

Let's go back to what we learned about dreams and goals and break it down.

Firstly, what does a career path as a financial analyst look like? What are the steps you have to take to get there? Do you have to attend college? Will you need to start with an internship or are there junior positions? What kind of institutions would you work at? What responsibilities would you have? What would your work hours be like?

Secondly, when you imagine living the life of a financial analyst—all the day-to-day work—is it still something you'd like to do? Financial analysts at big firms can be expected to work under a lot of pressure and have long days. The pay is usually good, though.

Lastly, consider if the chosen career will align with your values? Would you be happy to work at any firm/bank as a financial analyst, or would you only wish to work at certain firms whose values align with yours?

What do I mean by a business or firm having values?

It might be easier to explain with another example than the one above about becoming a financial analyst. Let's say you have a huge interest in military history and international relations, you love strategy and problem-solving, and are physically very active. That would, perhaps, make joining the military an interesting career option. Only, you don't believe in war. It goes against your values. So then you could consider becoming a peace negotiator instead.

Sometimes you have to think outside the box.

Make sure you understand that all career paths come with different considerations. Things like work hours, expected salary, and the various options for career growth once you land a job are all important things to consider. That's not to say that there aren't "unicorns." For example, while most entrepreneurs fail about three businesses before succeeding, work many hours per week, and earn a yearly income that isn't too impressive, some choose a very solid business idea, succeed right away, work a lot less hours, and make a lot more money.

Get the facts. Then dare to think outside the box.

Once you've decided what you want to do, turn it into a goal and start working towards it!

Oh, and one last thing—you can have more than one career. If you want to be an author, there's no saying you can't have a part-time job doing something else, for example. Or, if you want to start your own jewelry business selling things on Etsy, you can still have a "day job" until the business takes off. And there's no reason that day job should be boring.

People often think you have to "suffer" if you can't "live off your passion" right off the bat. There's no need. You can simply find a second career path you're really passionate about! This second career path might not be something you study at college, but there's no saying you can't take courses to learn a new skill.

KEY TAKEAWAYS

- To determine if a career path suits you, reflect on your skills and personality by answering relevant questions.
- If you're unsure about suitable careers that excite you, seek feedback from friends and family based on your answers.
- Consider using AI tools to brainstorm new career ideas based on your responses.
- Once you identify a potential career path, revisit the chapter on goals and dreams to assess if it's a genuine aspiration or just a fantasy.
- Understand the realities of the profession before committing to pursue it.
- If you decide to move forward, outline the steps needed to achieve your career goals and begin taking action.

✳ College Preparation ... or Choosing a Different Path

In high school, you usually study required subjects. In college, you get to study what you *want* to study, making studying potentially more enjoyable! However, college can also be a waste of time and money if it doesn't align with your goals.

Here are some things to consider when deciding on whether to attend college:

- Does my career path require college?
- Are there other reasons to attend college—such as creating a good social network and learning life skills?
- Can I still take courses for personal enrichment without committing to a degree?

- Would vocational courses or an apprenticeship be more helpful for my career?

College is not always a yes or no decision. Let's say you want to become a mechanic. You already know mechanics as you have family who are mechanics and you've been helping them since you were a kid. You still want to get a certificate to prove your skills, and you want to take a business course at college to meet more people and learn how to run your own business.

You don't have to get a certificate. You don't have to take a business course. But it will give you credentials and teach you things that are useful. You have to decide if that's important enough to spend the time and money needed for college.

Remember that education is not all about college, either; it involves developing skills like finding and questioning information, structuring thoughts, and building interpersonal skills. Research and feedback are essential parts of learning.

Education should empower you to make informed decisions rather than relying solely on your feelings. Engaging in new experiences and learning can provide a broader perspective on life.

If you decide to go to college, below are some things to consider.

✳ Academic Preparation

- Focus on maintaining strong grades but remember that extracurricular activities matter too.
- Prepare for standardized tests (note that requirements may differ internationally).
- Consider Advanced Placement (AP) or International Baccalaureate courses for college credit and better admission chances.
- Learn effective study and time management skills.

✳ Extracurricular Activities

- Join clubs and volunteer to enhance your college applications and develop skills.
- Taking on leadership roles can demonstrate your initiative.

✳ College Research

- Investigate colleges that align with your goals and interests, and if possible, visit campuses to gauge their atmosphere.
- Attend college fairs to gather direct information.

✳ Application Process

- Create a timeline for applications and deadlines.
- Write a compelling personal statement and gather letters of recommendation.
- Prepare a resume highlighting your achievements and experiences.

✳ Financial Preparation

- Research scholarships and grants early, and understand your financial aid options in your country.
- Create a budget for your college expenses.

✳ Personal Development

- Cultivate independence by learning life skills and managing time effectively.
- Prioritize self-care to maintain focus and well-being.

✳ Career Exploration

- Seek internships or part-time jobs during college to build experience and connections.
- Utilize career counseling resources if uncertain about your career path.
- Build a network through school and extracurricular organizations.

✳ College Life Skills

- Develop social skills and learn to communicate effectively with roommates.
- Familiarize yourself with campus resources.

Please be aware that not everything is about your grades. You can have average grades and still be accepted to a great college if you show you do personal projects or volunteer work that's extraordinary.

When looking at college options, consider that you might not want to attend a "top college." It usually comes with a heavy price tag. What you want is somewhere you will feel comfortable and happy, but that will also push you towards your goal, get you out of your comfort zone a bit, and make you grow! Of course, there's nothing wrong with top colleges though—you just have to find what works best for you!

Remember there are colleges overseas, too. I've attended school on three different continents, so I should know. Sometimes, it's actually cheaper, too. But then you have to factor in what it will be like being far from home.

Also, remember that you can take a gap year before college if you want to. Work. Travel. Do an apprenticeship. Just don't lose focus on getting into college the following year! Have clear goals for what you need to do to prepare for that, too.

In fact, if you don't get into your college of choice, you could try to get more experience during your gap year and apply again.

If you choose to take a gap year, be sure you know your purpose for it.

Have plans for your gap year and act on them! Of course, your plans can simply be to get a job and save up for college. Then do that. Don't get derailed by something else.

KEY TAKEAWAYS

- Education is essential for personal and professional development, and there are many pathways beyond traditional college, such as vocational courses, apprenticeships, and internships.
- Taking courses, even informally, can enhance your skills and career opportunities.
- Education broadens our understanding of the world, fosters critical thinking, and equips us with life skills, teaching us how to find and utilize information effectively.
- If you decide to attend college, create a step-by-step goal plan to navigate the application and enrollment process.
- If considering a gap year, plan activities that align with your interests and goals, whether it's improving college prospects, traveling, or gaining work experience.
- Use the gap year wisely to ensure it's a fulfilling experience rather than a period of aimlessness; reflect on what you truly want to achieve during this time.

✳ Leaving the Nest

Perhaps you won't go to college. Perhaps you'll go to college in a town where your family lives and stay at home to save money, or perhaps you want to stay at home because your family is epic. But sooner or later, no matter what path you take, you're going to leave home. Even if it's just to move across the street (which is really common in some cultures and can create a great support structure, while still giving you independence).

Moving away from home can be scary. Since I was fourteen, I attended courses and programs overseas, so I didn't find moving away from home one bit strange. I thought it was all a grand adventure. But I also experienced one trip I went on before leaving home that went terribly wrong and I came running back home.

Things happen. Needing your family is not a bad thing. You just have to, little by little, learn how to manage your own life. Because once you do, you feel free and powerful. You can still be as close to your family as you like, but you have the ability to stand on your own two legs.

There are things you can do leading to moving away from home that can help empower you:

- Learn how to manage a home: pay bills, plan meals, book appointments, do laundry (ask your parents or research if needed).
- Practice things you find uncomfortable, like making calls for appointments, while still at home.
- Plan how to fill your free time in ways that make you happy and help you meet new people when you move to a new place.
- Learn budgeting and start saving for emergencies.
- Attend a camp or take a course to experience time away from home with adult guidance.
- Try a weekend trip with friends to get a feel for independence.
- Explore new places on your own and practice navigating with GPS or maps.
- Prepare for self-care when you move by scheduling mood-boosting activities.
- Work on any personal skills, like improving confidence or social skills, before you leave.
- Ensure you feel safe by having emergency funds, a smoke alarm, personal safety items, and learning self-defense.
- Schedule regular video calls with family and friends when life gets busy after moving.
- Write a packing list based on where you'll be living—on campus, traveling, or living alone.

If you feel really nervous to move from home, consider seeing a counselor or therapist who can give you some tools to use. Just a few sessions with them can help calm your fears and allow you to step into your power! You can do this!

As always, remember to break things down. Do one thing at a time.

Also, when you do move, bear in mind that there will be days when you might miss home or feel lonely. It takes time to get to know a new place and meet new friends. Don't see it as a failure and think you'll always be miserable if things don't work out right away. This is also why it's important to schedule extracurricular activities you know you'll enjoy and time for self-care.

KEY TAKEAWAYS

Go through the bullet points in this chapter and create a plan. What are the things you're going to do to get ready to leave the nest?

Don't overwhelm yourself. Work on different things on different weeks.

Be prepared to enjoy yourself when you move, but also know there will be days when you will feel lost and lonely and that's okay. Fill your diary with things to do that will lift your spirits and let you meet other people. Also, set aside time for self-care—exercise, time in nature, and mindfulness exercises, among other things.

12 PERSONAL FINANCES

Finances can cause a lot of stress and a lot of joy. Let it be the latter. Because it's a lot more fun to live a life where you feel you have plenty and get to do the things you love! And responsible spending will lead to just that.

✴ The Very Basics of Budgeting

Budgeting is, in its most basic form, writing down all the costs you have for the month (it could be for a week, or year, but often you do monthly budgeting, as well as looking at the entire year to plan for certain costs) and then comparing your estimates to how much you spent.

You have to put down all the essentials when budgeting. Essentials are the things you have to cover to get by, such as rent, food, toiletries, electricity, Wi-Fi, medical insurance, car payments, gas, college fees, etc.

Then there are things you might not buy on a monthly basis but that you also need to have money set aside for, such as haircuts, shoes, clothes, makeup, stationery, visits to the doctor, Christmas gifts, trips, etc.

You also put down costs for "extras," such as entertainment and snacks that you don't really need (such as grabbing a coffee in the cafeteria).

Why do we do budgeting? Because we want to know that we don't spend money on unnecessary things.

Consider that coffee in the cafeteria.

It's just a cup of coffee. No big deal. Just five bucks, let's say.

If you do that every day, five days a week, it's $25 per week, $100 per month (if we round it off as a month isn't exactly four weeks), and $1,200 per year.

Things add up.

One bar of chocolate here, a cinema ticket there, and suddenly ... the money's gone. Even though you didn't do anything. You didn't buy a new wardrobe or take a trip to Spain.

This is why it's important to have a budget and track where your money is going.

KEY TAKEAWAYS

- A budget is a financial plan that outlines projected income and expenses over a specific period.
- It aids in effective money management by tracking spending and meeting financial goals while avoiding overspending.
- Budget for infrequent expenses (e.g., haircuts) even if they're not monthly.
- It helps prevent excessive spending on unnecessary small items, as these can accumulate to significant amounts over time.

✳ Understanding Why You Need a Safety Net

Everything is going fine until the washing machine breaks, the car tires need changing, you fracture your arm, and suddenly, there's no money to pay the bills.

You've budgeted. You've covered your monthly costs brilliantly. You've even saved a bit of money towards a trip next summer. Now that money's gone, you're broke, and you don't have a washing machine.

This is why you need a safety net.

Sometimes it can be hard to save up for a safety net. Especially if you don't earn much more than you need. But even if you're just saving one dollar a day, try to do so. Because one day, you'll need it.

This is also why insurance is so important. It feels horrible paying every month for something, but the day something goes wrong, if it goes wrong, there's someone there to pay for it. And some things can get ridiculously expensive, such as legal matters or healthcare.

You can be fit as a fiddle and still break an arm in two places or have someone try to defraud you and be forced to pay for a lawyer that costs a fortune.

Life throws us screwballs and insurance helps us handle them!

KEY TAKEAWAYS

When you budget, bear in mind that you need to put money away for things you will need at a certain date in the future. Dentist and doctor appointments, replacing things and repairing things, accidents, and so forth.

Insurance is also really important. It can cover extreme costs, such as surgery, rebuilding your home after a fire, or having your things stolen during a break in.

✳ Spending and Saving Jars

As part of budgeting and saving, it's good to understand the concept of jars.

Basically, jars are like piggy banks for different things. One is for monthly costs, one for investments, one for emergency costs, and so forth. *Every time you get paid, you divide the money you receive between your different jars.*

And in a moment, you'll see how easy it makes your life!

The first jar is always day-to-day costs that need to be covered. So before you create the jars, make a budget, as discussed in the first part of this chapter. Then, once you've worked out how much money you need to get by, you'll know what you have left for other things.

Let's say you're being paid $2,500 per month.

- **Jar One: Monthly Basic Costs ($1,800):** You can divide this into different jars if you want to see your monthly budget more clearly, like have one for rent, one for bills, one for food, etc.
- **Jar Two: Emergency Savings ($125)**
- **Jar Three: Short-Term Savings ($100):** Buying a new phone, going for a weekend getaway, getting an expensive pair of shoes, etc.
- **Jar Four: Long-Term Savings ($200):** Buying a car, a home, going on a longer vacation, etc.
- **Jar Five: Investments ($200)**
- **Jar Six: Charity ($25)**
- **Jar Seven: Happy Days Fund ($25):** Random stuff.
- **Jar Eight: Retirement Fund ($25)**

As you age and things change, the numbers in the jars will change. Right now, your retirement fund is not a priority, but it will become so as you get older and have a better income.

You can have more jars than in this example, and you can have less, but I believe the eight jars above cover the main things.

Can you see that dividing your money this way as soon as you receive them will help stop you from spending them on things you don't really need? And ensuring, instead, that you always have money for the things you need?

What's more, it ensures you have money to do fun things when you want to, instead of spending loose change on coffees.

I always wish someone would have taught me this when I was in my teens! It would have saved me a lot of headache.

Some banks these days actually allow you to have jars so that you can have different jars within the same account. Not all banks allow this, but you can open a bank account for each jar instead!

What if you don't earn enough to save?

Still set up the jars. Then start by putting nominal amounts in them each month. As you earn more, you can increase the sums.

Also, remember that the day when the washing machine breaks will come. So if you aren't earning enough money to save for this, what will you do? You can perhaps use a credit card to buy a new washing machine, but how will you pay that off if you aren't earning more than you spend?

If you feel you can't save anything at all, consider getting an extra job or finding one that pays better. Also, see if there are items on your current budget that you can cut.

KEY TAKEAWAYS

- Dividing money into jars or bank accounts as soon as you receive it helps prevent unnecessary spending and provides clarity on where your money goes.
- This method allows for saving for future needs.
- Even if income is low, start by saving a dollar or two to develop the habit, and increase amounts as earnings grow.
- If unable to save due to low income, consider taking an extra job, finding better-paying work, or reducing current expenses.

✳ The Very Basics of Investments

You might be convinced that investments will either lose you money or make you very rich. The truth? It depends on how you invest.

Here are some very basic tips for investment. I'm not giving you financial advice, just sharing things you should know as you think about money and investments.

- There are different kinds of investments—you can put your money into businesses, stocks, art, or even crypto.
- Never put in money you can't afford to say goodbye to.
- If one investment doesn't do well, having others can help protect your money.
- Some investments, like buying stocks, are about waiting and hoping the company gets better over time. Others, like day trading, involve constantly buying and selling, which can be a lot of work.
- Some bank accounts let you earn interest just for keeping your money there, but it may not be a lot. It's called **compound interest**, which means you earn interest on the money you earn over time!

- Not everything you own is an investment. For example, cars usually lose value, but things like collectible items can become more valuable.
- Always read up on things you're interested in investing in and ask for help if you're confused.

Having a small pool of your savings set aside for different investments can be a great way of earning some extra money, though it always comes with risk.

If you want to invest, watch some YouTube videos, read a couple of blogs, and then get some books on the topic. You might even consider meeting with a trusted financial advisor. By easing your way into it, it won't feel overwhelming, but rather you will feel empowered as you learn how to take charge of your money!

Please note that there is good and bad information out there. Don't just look at one source. You have to explore different sources.

KEY TAKEAWAYS

- Investment basics are straightforward, and even small amounts can significantly impact your financial future.
- Diversifying investments is crucial; consider a mix of risky investments for quick returns and long-term investments (like property) for stability and growth over time.
- Start educating yourself on investment strategies with easy-to-digest resources like videos and blogs before moving on to books and online courses.
- Research online courses to ensure they have positive reviews before enrolling.
- Consult a reputable financial advisor to gain personalized insights and guidance.

PART 4:

Global Citizenship and Entering the World Stage

13 GLOBAL CITIZENSHIP AND COMMUNITY

Community is super important. And today, not everything is about your local community. Through social media, businesses, and other means of connecting, we are tying ties globally.

✳ Global Citizenship

We no longer live in one little corner of a country where we have no interaction with the rest of the world. The Internet and airplanes changed all of that. As did world trade. When was the last time you used something from China or India, for example?

Today?

Yesterday?

And your favorite store might just be owned by a company that has stores in many different countries.

We're interconnected these days. Stuff happening in one country affects other countries as we are all connected through trade, international businesses, and various organizations.

Plus, through the Internet, you likely interact with people from other countries all the time.

A few decades ago, people outside of India had very little idea of what people in India watched when going to the movies or on TV. Now, you can find Bollywood pictures on Netflix and other platforms.

And it's not just that you can watch movies from other countries, you can look at people's social media feeds, read their blogs, even call them over WhatsApp, Zoom, Skype, Messenger, or whatever other app you might be using.

We're simply reaching a point where we're all interconnected.

Many people today encourage this connected Earth and see themselves as global citizens as opposed to being the citizens of just one country. Not least because it's become so much easier to go to different countries and even live there.

As work becomes more and more remote, we also have the opportunity to work from countries we aren't even employed in and with international teams. Plus, a business you work at in one country might very well open its doors in another country, giving you an opportunity to move there. You also have the opportunity to study at schools abroad—most countries offer student visas.

As a result of people moving about more, different cultures come into contact and even merge.

If you want to travel and explore the world, it's a great time for it! But also bear in mind that even if you don't travel, the global landscape will affect you.

KEY TAKEAWAYS

Thanks to more effective and cheaper means of travel, global trade, international businesses, and the Internet, the world is more interconnected than ever before.

As a result of this trend of globalization, a lot of people these days consider themselves global citizens—recognizing that we're all part of a whole, even if we have different cultures.

✳ Cultural Sensitivity

Do you remember your grandmother, mother, or father telling you that something was a certain way?

"You don't disobey the elderly." (But sometimes the elderly can be mistaken.)

"Never eat dinner in your pajamas. It'll offend the cook, who is usually your mom." (In some families, eating in your pajamas is perfectly fine.)

"People who pray tend to live happier lives." (Maybe they do! There's actually research about the benefits of prayer, but surely there are many different ways to be happy.)

"Cows are holy." (This is true in Hinduism.)

"Cows are food." (This is true for people who eat beef.)

These statements represent beliefs rather than facts. They are things we grow up believing in, or not believing in, depending on where we were raised and who raised us.

We all carry these beliefs with us, which can influence many aspects of our lives, including the way we dress, our sense of humor, our moral beliefs, and so much more.

In the book *Sapiens*, Yuval Noah Harari talks about how human beliefs have changed through the centuries.

For instance, in 19th century England, many people believed your social class was decided at birth, and changing that was thought to go against divine order. Marrying outside your class was often frowned upon, especially for women, whose reputations could be at stake for actions that men wouldn't face the same scrutiny for.

These historical views often stemmed from the practical realities of the time. Women, particularly from upper classes, had limited job opportunities and relied on marriage for financial security, which added to the pressure to conform to certain standards of behavior.

Looking back, we can see that ideas of "civilization" varied greatly. For example, some cultures once believed it was their duty to expand their territory, which today raises questions about morality and ethics.

Beliefs and customs, whether they seem good or bad, often come from the context in which we live. What is considered honorable in one culture may seem strange or even wrong in another.

Cultural traditions are rich and varied, from the food we eat to the music we listen to. Before judging someone's "strange clothes," remember that your outfit might seem just as unusual to them!

Take the example of holiday traditions. In Sweden, people decorate with straw goats for Yule, because of a myth about goats delivering gifts. In America, it's called Christmas, and gifts are delivered by a man who flies across the skies with his reindeer. Both customs might seem odd, but they are meaningful to those who celebrate them.

As you meet people from different cultures, you may find that some of your beliefs are just that—beliefs. Engaging with diverse perspectives can lead to questioning your own views, which can be a valuable experience.

Respect is crucial. If you enter another culture believing that your way is the only way, it can be offensive and can hinder potential friendships. Yes, some people choose vegetarianism, while others enjoy different cuisines, but at our core, we all want to feel loved, secure, and enjoy good food together.

When you meet someone from another culture, be open to learning from their experiences instead of judging them based on your own background. This is becoming increasingly important as our world connects more and more. Embracing diversity enriches our lives, and understanding different beliefs is vital for success in schools and workplaces where diverse cultures come together.

Try to connect with others and discover what you have in common. As the saying goes, "You have to walk a mile in someone else's shoes to understand them." Doing so can broaden your perspective.

Keep in mind that if someone has traveled far to be in your country, they might be feeling a mix of excitement and nervousness. While their customs may seem unfamiliar, remember that your habits might feel just as odd to them!

Exploring new places can be daunting but also incredibly fun!

Lastly, it's important not to assume that someone's upbringing defines who they are. Yes, culture shapes us, but personal experiences also play a significant role. You might not fit every stereotype associated with your background!

Be mindful of biases and avoid making generalizations. Each person is unique, shaped by their culture but also by their individual experiences.

KEY TAKEAWAYS

- Cultural upbringing shapes our views on what is considered normal, including manners, dress, and beliefs.
- Recognizing our shared humanity despite cultural differences fosters connections with diverse individuals.
- Sensitivity to other cultures is essential in a globalized world; respect for differing beliefs (e.g., dietary restrictions) is crucial in the workplace.
- Building respectful relationships allows for learning and growth, challenging our long-held perceptions.
- Embracing diverse perspectives can be humbling and expand our understanding of the world.

✳ Why Sustainability Matters

Your body is an ecosystem. If you mess with the brain, you mess with the rest of the body. If you mess with a kidney, you mess with the rest of the body. Everything is interlinked, and each part affects the whole.

It's the same with the world. The world is a big place, and small changes might not have a great impact. But a lot of small changes or one big change certainly has a huge impact.

It's easy to think that our actions don't matter, but they do. Because a lot of small actions add up. For example, imagine if everyone decided to buy just *one* organic apple per year. That's about 8.2 billion apples. Meaning, 8.2 billion apples that weren't sprayed with any potentially toxic substances.

Never think your actions don't matter, because if everyone takes just one good action, it has a huge effect.

So what does it mean to lead a sustainable life? The United Nations (UN) defined it as "meeting the needs of the present without compromising the ability of future generations to meet their own needs."

In more general terms, when you talk about something being sustainable, it means it can support itself. A business is not sustainable if it costs more to operate than what it brings in, in revenue. The Earth is not sustainable if we're using up resources at such a rate they will be depleted.

Oxford Languages defines *sustainable* as "the ability to be maintained at a certain rate or level" or "avoidance of the depletion of natural resources in order to maintain an ecological balance."

It makes sense that we should want to take care of the world, because we need it to survive. If we run out of food, clean water, or electricity, what will we do? If the oceans become polluted or too hot, which disrupts the coral reefs, which disrupts oxygen production, what do we do?

If we start getting toxins in our food and water, what will we do? Well, we will become sick, or infertile, if the doses are high enough, that's what.

And even if it doesn't happen in our generation, what will become of our children and all the plants and animals that share this world with us in the next generation? Even if "it's just a plant that goes extinct," what if that plant holds the cure for cancer?

Stress on the Earth disrupts the Earth's systems and causes havoc. Because when one thing is affected, other things are affected. It's like the domino effect—once you hit one domino, they all go down. The Earth isn't as easy to manipulate as a set of dominoes, however. The Earth is resilient. Just like your body, it can overcome stress. But you have to give it a break to be able to do so.

The problem with pollution and resources would be really easy to solve if there weren't so many of us, but as the human population has grown dramatically since the industrial revolution due to better living standards and healthcare, we're in a position where we have got to start thinking about how we use our resources.

In fact, some resources are already starting to run out. Others are polluted. People around the globe, as well as plants and animals, are already suffering because of the environmental havoc we're causing.

It's time to start acting. Actually, it was time to start acting a long time ago. But that time has passed and there's no point mourning the past. The important thing is to *act now*.

So what can you do to "go green"?

Here are a few ideas (perhaps you can think of a few more?):

1. **Collect and Use Rainwater:** Install systems to collect rainwater for bathing and flushing toilets.

2. **Conserve Water:** Take short showers, don't fill the bathtub all the way, and take cold or colder showers occasionally.

3. **Use Eco-Friendly Products:** Opt for organic cotton pads and tampons, or use reusable items like the moon cup and reusable diapers washed in an eco-friendly manner.

4. **Sustainable Transportation:** Bike or walk whenever possible and use public transport to reduce carbon emissions.

5. **Energy-Efficient Lighting:** Use LED lamps or solar-charged lamps to save energy.

6. **Solar-Powered Devices:** Use devices powered by solar energy, such as solar battery banks.

7. **Eco-Friendly Fashion and Home Decor:** Buy organic and eco-friendly clothing and home decor items. Buy second hand or trade so that old products can be reused, and when you're done with your products, instead of trashing them, see if there are local charities or upcycling projects who want them (or upcycle yourself by turning them into something different).

8. **Reduce Plastic Use:** Avoid single-use plastics by using reusable bags, bottles, and containers (but don't compound the problem by buying too many reusable items).

9. **Compost:** Start composting food scraps and organic waste to reduce landfill use and create nutrient-rich soil.

10. **Plant a Garden:** Grow your own fruits, vegetables, and herbs to reduce your carbon footprint.

Look, you might not be able to do all the above—we don't all have the time or space to plant a garden, for example. Simply do what you can.

What do you think the future of sustainability will look like? For example, we have libraries for books, we can share bikes in cities where bikes are parked a bit here and there and everywhere, and new carpooling initiatives are popping up. Do you think there'll be other businesses where you share your things or borrow instead of own?

What do you think clothes will be like? All natural fibers? All recycled materials? Or fabric that contains solar cells to collect energy? And yes, all of that is already happening. So what's next?

There are also new organizations that pop up all the time, working to make businesses more sustainable. I've heard of incredible initiatives, like the Ellen MacArthur Foundation that works to create a circular economy. In their own words:

"The circular economy is a system where materials never become waste and nature is regenerated. In a circular economy, products and materials are kept in circulation through processes like maintenance, reuse, refurbishment, remanufacture, recycling, and composting. The circular economy tackles climate change and other global challenges, like biodiversity loss, waste, and pollution, by decoupling economic activity from the consumption of finite resources."

In nature, there is a natural circular economy if you think about food, for example. A rabbit eats a carrot, then poops out the leftovers, which is broken down into nutrients for the field, so that more plants can grow. Nothing is wasted.

Humans have, to an extent, disrupted that system. So now we have to look for ways where we become as smart as nature. And as science evolves, I'm sure we will find ways. With the advent of AI, we have incredible resources at our fingertips. If we can learn to use all the resources for good, and not just to enhance our own life or the amount of money our business makes, we can create miracles.

You live in an exciting time.

And if you have a moment, do some research. Find out about initiatives around sustainability and a circular economy. See what inventions are in the works. Get inspired. Then do some brainstorming—what exciting things do you think you'll see in your lifetime that will lead to a more sustainable Earth? And what can you do to help things along?

KEY TAKEAWAYS

- The Earth functions as an interconnected ecosystem; disruptions can have widespread effects.
- Human population growth and industrial advancements have significantly impacted nature.
- Sustainability means maintaining balance, allowing the Earth to regenerate at the same rate resources are depleted.
- The circular economy concept, promoted by the Ellen MacArthur Foundation, is built on three principles: eliminating waste and pollution, circulating products at their highest value, and regenerating nature.

- Staying informed about sustainability trends can inspire you to start a business, conduct research, or apply sustainable practices in your profession.
- Small actions contribute to sustainability; collective efforts can lead to significant impact (e.g., buying organic apples or recycling bottles).
- Every individual's actions matter; there are simple steps everyone can take to support the health of the planet.

14 TAKING CHARGE

There comes a day when you become the master of your own life ... so how do you become the leader you need to be when that day comes? In previous chapters, you've learned tools that can help you as a teenager and in adult life. This chapter is about becoming the leader who implements those tools by leading yourself and others.

✳ Leadership

Taking charge ... don't we all dream of that moment? The moment when we are free to do whatever we want and go out there and live our life to the full?

Actually, no. Some people don't feel like "natural born leaders." But even if you do, chances are you don't know how to be a great leader right off the bat.

The thing is, we're all leaders. No, you might not be the captain of the netball team, the head of your local choir, or the CEO of the next billion-dollar tech company. But you lead yourself in everyday life—you have to take charge of your life.

Besides, in our work and our personal life, there are times where we have to lead, even if we aren't the leader of the project, the boss, or whatever. Don't you lead your aging parents? Don't you lead your colleagues when you start an initiative to do something fun for everyone's birthday? Or gather funds to buy something for someone who is sick? Yes, you do. You lead.

You also lead when you make yourself do your homework, or get your kids ready for school.

So what does it mean to be a leader?

Leadership is the ability to guide, inspire, and influence others (or yourself!) to achieve a common goal. It involves creating a vision, making decisions, and motivating people to work together effectively. Leadership isn't just about holding a position of authority; it's about making a positive impact and fostering a collaborative environment.

And let's look at the bit about the common goal here: leadership is about enrolling other people in your vision. You need to get them on board. And not by manipulating them. Share your vision and see if it's for them. You need to speak to their hearts—if it rings true for them, they will join you and work *alongside* you.

Trying to get the wrong people to join your crew is an awful idea. It's going to lead to everyone being unhappy. So be honest, but also really reach people's hearts. A lot of people have no idea how good it feels to do good for others, for example. If you can inspire them by sharing what good it did you, you might help them find something that will not only serve others but will also serve them.

Likewise, people might be totally unaware of some green initiative that could change the world, or some disease that is affecting people badly, or the team of researchers that needs funds to be able to find a cure or alleviate symptoms.

Before you enroll others in a vision, or even create one for yourself, go back and look at the sections about dreams and goals, as well as decision-making. Do your research. Ask your intuition. Figure out if you truly want to lead a project and why.

Key Leadership Qualities

1. **Communication:** Effective leaders communicate clearly and listen actively. They express their ideas confidently and encourage an open dialogue.
2. **Empathy:** Understanding and caring about the needs and feelings of others helps build strong relationships. You can't successfully lead others if you ignore *their* needs.
3. **Integrity:** Being honest, ethical, and consistent in your actions earns respect and trust from others.

4. **Resilience:** Leaders face challenges head-on and remain determined and optimistic, even in difficult situations.

5. **Adaptability:** Being open to change and able to adjust strategies as needed is crucial in a fast-paced world. Remember the section about roadblocks?

6. **Vision:** Great leaders have a clear vision of what they want to achieve and can inspire others to share and pursue that vision.

7. **Confidence:** Not the cocky "I know I'm right" kind of confidence, but genuinely being okay in who you are and willing to *adjust as you gather new facts.* You have to be willing to take on feedback, adapt, and grow if you want to be a great leader. Which is the total opposite of "my way or the highway." You're leading others on your way, so you have to constantly ensure it's the best way to go!

Remember, no matter what you do, you'll make mistakes. Don't let that get you down. I've directed plays extremely well. I've also done a variety show that was so crap I thought I'd sink through the floor in humiliation. I did it on the request of a friend, and we didn't have enough time to rehearse together. When I saw the show from start to finish, it was an assembly of mismatched acts.

I remember waking up the next day thinking I wanted to hide under the blankets. But as a good director, I knew what the issues were and how to fix them. And I learned that putting together a show like that without rehearsals didn't work—you'd have to know the acts up front and that they'd work well together.

You learn. You move on to the next project. Or you sit feeling embarrassed for the rest of your life. Just learn from it and then focus on what you can do next.

What are some steps to develop leadership skills?

1 **Start Early:** Take on leadership roles in school or community activities. Start small, like organizing family events, and build from there.

2 **Learn from Role Models:** Observe leaders you admire, whether teachers, coaches, or peers, and note their unique strengths.

3 **Practice Decision-Making:** Make thoughtful choices and take responsibility for the outcomes. Learn from mistakes without stressing over them.

4 **Work on Communication:** Practice clear speaking and active listening. Participate more at home, in class, or in clubs.

5 **Be a Team Player:** Collaborate with others, share credit, and support your peers. Leadership is about teamwork, not just being in charge.

6 **Set Goals:** Create personal and group goals, plan how to achieve them, and inspire others to join you.

7 **Seek Feedback and Learn:** Ask for feedback from mentors and be open to learning new skills through workshops or self-study.

8 **Stay Positive:** Maintain a positive attitude even during challenges. Your optimism can uplift others and make the journey more enjoyable.

9 **Volunteer:** Engage in community service to build leadership and teamwork skills while helping others.

10 **Know Your Strengths and Support Others:** Understand your own strengths and weaknesses. Recognize others' talents and let them shine when needed.

Of course, you have to lead by example, too. Demonstrate the values and behaviors you expect from others. Show respect, work hard, and treat people with kindness. When you lead by example, you inspire others to follow suit.

Let's come back to the challenges.

Every leader faces challenges. It's important to

- **Stay Calm:** Approach problems with a clear mind and avoid panic.
- **Analyze the Situation:** Understand the issue fully before taking action.

- **Seek Solutions:** Focus on finding solutions rather than dwelling on problems.
- **Involve Others:** Collaborate with your team to brainstorm and implement solutions.

Good leaders can make a significant positive impact on their communities, organizations, and the world. The sooner you start to develop leadership skills, the further you'll get. And as mentioned, it's also about leading yourself and your own life.

Just bear in mind you don't have to lead large projects if that's not your thing. Try to come up with things you can do to lead a team that you are comfortable with, such as organizing an outing with friends.

Lastly, look at the bullet points in this chapter and think about how you can use these points, not just to lead others, but to lead yourself. Do you have empathy when it comes to yourself? Do you have resilience? Do you ask for feedback? Are you adaptable?

KEY TAKEAWAYS

- Leadership goes beyond managing large projects; it's about self-leadership and everyday initiatives, like organizing a trip with friends.
- Effective leadership involves engaging others in a shared vision and taking action to realize that vision.
- Key qualities of a good leader include clear communication, empathy, integrity, resilience, adaptability, a strong vision, confidence, and a commitment to personal growth.
- Understanding your strengths and weaknesses, as well as those of your team, is essential for effective collaboration.
- Steps to becoming a great leader include practicing decision-making, enhancing communication skills, being a team player, setting goals, seeking feedback, maintaining a positive attitude, and being open to continuous learning.

✳ Stepping Out of Your Comfort Zone

The life you want is usually outside your comfort zone.

For example, due to a few plot twists in my childhood, I became very shy. I realized that fear was holding me back—I wasn't speaking my mind or acting as I'd like. I prevented myself from being who I am because I was scared of people's opinions. So I decided I'd speak even though I was petrified.

I didn't have to do that once. I had to do that over and over and over again until I became comfortable with doing it. And it's not like I started out being the life of the party. I took a lot of very small steps to eventually turn into the woman I am today.

I remember reading Tim Ferriss' book *The 4-Hour Work Week*. In it, he shares that he went around striking up conversations with women in shopping malls to get over his fear of doing it. Sometimes it went well, sometimes it didn't. Eventually, it became second nature.

Once we have confidence, we don't really care if things go wrong sometimes. We know it will go wrong. It's okay. It will go right, too.

When we're scared, we interpret everything as a failure. And we make that failure *mean things about us.* "If people look at me funny when I speak, it means I can't make friends and something must be terribly wrong with me. Perhaps I am just unlovable."

> If you are to grow, you have to step out of your comfort zone and be willing to make mistakes.

For example, I recently put in a pitch for a job I was uncertain I could do. It was copywriting for a crypto site.

I do lots of copywriting, but I knew next to nothing about crypto.

I looked at their branding and the wireframes they had for the site.

I wasn't too fond of the branding. A bit dull.

Then I decided I was going to get that job. *I committed to my goal.* I read through all their financial documents and asked ChatGPT about everything I did not understand.

I created a mockup of the landing page. I got on a call with the client and told them straight up I know nothing about crypto.

I got the job.

I got to rework their branding.

The team is awesome. They love explaining everything so I get to learn.

I now have a new project from the same client. Also in finance. Another thing I'm going to have to learn.

I was uncomfortable during this process, but I got a job that has turned into a dream job. I'm having fun, and I'm learning.

If you want to achieve your goals and reach your dreams, chances are you are going to have to do things that freak you out. But as I said—do them enough times and they stop being freaky. They become normal. Then you move on to the next level. Try something else that's a bit freaky.

And, as always, break it down. Do it step by step. If the idea of talking to people in shopping malls scares the living daylights out of you, start with giving shop assistants you speak with when buying something compliments. I used to do that. I still do. If there's a possibility to say something nice to someone, do it. That's your power—you can give them something good just using your words.

If you want to up your game, you have to step out of your comfort zone but do so in a manner that you can handle. Doing too much, too soon, will only lead to failure. But doing something small that you can handle will increase your confidence. Yes, you'll fail sometimes, but the more you do it, the better you'll get, even if it's uncomfortable at first.

It's like cold baths—one does not always want to step into them, but boy does it feel good when one gets out!

And if you want to get to the next level in life, you have to do something you haven't yet done. That's usually a little bit frightening, but also exciting.

KEY TAKEAWAYS

- To grow and evolve, you must consistently challenge yourself to try new things.
- Start with small steps, like improving your cooking skills through new recipes or techniques.
- Larger challenges, such as going on a first date, can also be part of your growth journey.
- New experiences may feel intimidating; find ways to break them down into manageable steps.
- For instance, socialize more to build confidence in your conversational skills, making a date feel less daunting.

✳ Innovative Thinking

I love innovative thinking. Is there anything more creatively juicy than thinking outside the box? Coming up with new solutions? Problem solving?

I don't think so. But then, I'm not you. You might like to organize and plan ahead, play it safe and play by the rules. We all have different super powers. But we can all learn to see the world, and problems, from different perspectives.

In one of the coaching programs I attended, I did an exercise where we were asked to write down at least ten solutions to what we considered a problem.

When you have a problem, consider trying this out. Give yourself ten minutes to come up with ten different solutions. Start with anything you can think of, even the most incredible, insane, and unlikely solution (such as winning $10M on the lottery, or running into Richard Branson or Taylor Swift and asking for the same). Once done, look at the list of solutions. From that list, something is likely to jump out at you.

Why do you include insanely unlikely solutions? Because usually we limit our thinking by considering only what *we* think is possible. By including all sorts of random solutions, we look at the problem from new angles and we often get ideas for how to actually solve it.

Doing this exercise, we were taught there's at least three solutions to every unsolvable problem.

I don't know how true that is, but once you look at a problem both logically and by throwing any random solution you can think of into the mix, you start seeing things in new ways.

Another way of tackling problems is to meditate. Sleep. Go do something else. Your mind works in incredible ways. Decide you'll find a solution, then let your brain find it in its own time. You can do this after brainstorming, then your mind will sort things out, see the patterns and so forth.

If you can't find a solution? Ask friends and family. Ask Google. Ask AI. Ask the experts. Pester every person you can think of and a few that you think are totally unlikely to have an answer. Because answers pop up in the most unlikely of places.

Everything's impossible until it's done. There was a time when so many things we do today were thought of as impossible. Imagine telling someone in the 1400s that you can write something and share it with people all over the world without having to walk to each person's house. Thanks to the Internet, we can do that today. However, to get to the point where we were able to invent the Internet, we first had to discover and invent a series of other things so as to be able to conceive the idea.

Personally, I still find the Internet and AI totally mind blowing.

Never think of something as being impossible to do. Something might turn out not to be the right thing for you, but don't give up because you face a problem. Give up because you can see it's a waste of your time and energy. It's not right for you.

Problems are juicy. They are fun little riddles to solve. A game to play. Don't get your knickers in a twist about it, as the British say (isn't that just a brilliant expression?).

KEY TAKEAWAYS

- Most challenges can be tackled; brainstorm all possible solutions, no matter how outlandish.
- Reviewing your list of ideas may reveal a feasible solution or a step toward finding one.
- Involving others can provide new perspectives and insights you might not have considered.
- A strong motivation for your goal can increase your commitment and drive to find solutions.
- Take breaks from problem-solving; activities like meditation, walking, or sleeping allow your brain to process and connect ideas subconsciously.

In Closing

Do you feel empowered having read this book? Or does it all seem like too much?

If it seems like too much, don't worry.

Re-read all the key takeaways. Go back and do the different exercises in the various chapters. Always remember to break things down and tackle one thing at a time. In fact, you can focus on implementing just one chapter a week, or month.

On the flip side, does what you've read about seem like a piece of cake? You already mastered it all? Great. Go out and seek more knowledge. Think about sharing your knowledge with others.

There's so much to life. We're constantly learning and evolving if we want to be. It's exciting. And as I've mentioned in this book, we mustn't take it personally if we sometimes make mistakes or fail at things. That's what you do while you learn.

Life is a constant rollercoaster where you go up and down. The more wisdom you have, the more balanced things become, but there will never be a flat road forward unless you sit in bed doing nothing.

If you're having a bad time, relax. Know that good times will come. Keep moving forward.

If you're having a great time, enjoy it while also continuing to build a community around you—a support network—and moving forward at school, or your professional career, while also saving up funds. That way, when there's a bump in the road, you have the resources you need to get through.

Always remember the mood booster exercises and have a routine that fosters your mental well-being. This will help balance out the ups and downs.

Don't ever be scared to reach out for help, whether hiring a therapist to assist you in building your confidence and life skills, or a professional to help you with something practical, like your finances. And when you get stuck with things, ask around. Friends and family are often more than happy to help so long as you're also willing to help them.

None of us can do this thing called life alone. Or perhaps we can, but it's a lot easier with assistance and usually takes us a lot further. Plus, it's more fun.

You can do this. You have everything you need within you to lead a life you love. It's not always going to be easy, but it's going to be filled with moments of joy, beauty, love, friendship, exhilaration, and gorgeousness! I'm not sure you can say it will be filled with gorgeousness, but I'll say it anyway. Because life can be pretty darn gorgeous!

Made in United States
Troutdale, OR
12/28/2024

27370625R00116